TRINITY
STUDENT
PRANKS

TRINITY STUDENT PRANKS

A History of Mischief & Mayhem

John Engle

The History Press Ireland

To the Noonans:
Adam, Joe, Niamh, Rebecca and Oscar.
For Edward Byron Smith, Jr and Maureen Dwyer Smith.
For my father and mother, who brought me up to
appreciate mischief in all its forms.
And for Caoimhe.

First published 2013

The History Press Ireland
50 City Quay
Dublin 2
Ireland
www.thehistorypress.ie

British Library Cataloguing in Publication Data.
A catalogue record for this book is available from the British Library.

ISBN 978 1 84588 795 7

Typesetting and origination by The History Press

CONTENTS

	Acknowledgements	6
	Introduction	7
1.	The Birth of a University and of Prankery	11
2.	The Golden Age of Mayhem: Trinity in the Eighteenth Century	16
3.	Guns, Ghosts and Tall Tales	24
4.	A Prankster's Guide to Trinity College	31
5.	Political Mischief	39
6.	Battle on the Quad	46
7.	Lads of the Boat Club	55
8.	Over (and Up) the Walls	58
9.	The Prince of Mischief and the Great Dean	73
10.	The Women of Trinity	83
11.	Ancient Rivalry, Modern Mischief: The Old Societies of College	89
12.	If You Can't Win, Steal	101
13.	Arena of Mayhem: The Colours Debates	110
14.	Myths and Legends	118
	Epilogue: The Future of Mischief	124

ACKNOWLEDGEMENTS

I would like to thank several people without whose help this book would not have been finished: Patrick Geoghegan, Ciaran Denny, Caoimhe Stafford, Kate Brady, Liam Brophy, Siobhan and Clyde Engle, Peter Henry, Eoghan Casey, Howard Helen, Fletch Williams, the University Philosophical Society, Glen Rogers, Aifric Ní Chriodain, Andrea Waitz, David Barrett, Eoin O'Liathain, Fergus Rattigan, Lorcan Clarke, David McConnell, Alison McIntyre, Paul Logue, Jamie Donnelly, Lorcan Cullen, Ricky McCormack, David Byrne, Michael Wycherley, Brent Northup, Ruth Faller, Ciara Finlay, David Barrett, James Doyle, Shane Glackin, Cormac McGuinness, Lorcan Cullen, Thomas Kinsella.

INTRODUCTION

Trinity College Dublin is the oldest and finest university in Ireland. Founded in 1592 by Queen Elizabeth I, Trinity has developed over more than four centuries into one of the world's foremost institutions of higher education. One of the seven ancient universities of the English-speaking world, it has produced countless illustrious graduates, from authors such as Oscar Wilde, Bram Stoker and Samuel Beckett, to scientists like Ernest Walton. Trinity truly has become synonymous with its elaborate buildings and the storied men and women who populate them.

Nestled in the heart of Dublin, Trinity is an oasis of scholarship. When one passes through its front arch, one immediately feels a change of pace, as the noise of the city is drowned out by the thick walls and even thicker patina of tradition and scholarship. Tourists flock from around the world to visit Trinity's historic buildings and world-famous library, which houses the elaborate *Book of Kells*.

Yet the tourists only get to hear one part of the story. Outside Trinity's formal histories and public-relations efforts runs a different history, a history of mischief and mayhem.

For Trinity has produced not only the finest scholars, thinkers, and doers on the Emerald Isle, but also clever and talented pranksters.

Queen Elizabeth I. Founder of the University, Elizabeth sought to create a bastion of learning to shore up the rule of her Protestant monarchy. (Wikimedia Commons)

The *Book of Kells*. Trinity is perhaps best known as the institution housing the *Book of Kells*, the world's greatest example of illuminated manuscripts. (Wikimedia Commons)

This book seeks to fill a gap in the history of Trinity College by telling the tales of the great masters of mischief who have over the centuries populated its ranks. Their story, in many ways, tells the story of the college itself, by highlighting the

The Main Façade. Facing out on College Green, Trinity College is nestled right in the centre of Dublin. (Aifric Ní Chríodáin)

mores and attitudes of young people on the ground level. Rather than pursuing the narrow course of history in a completely straight line, the following chapters are laid out in such a way as to group together stories of similar topic, while also following Time's Arrow as much as is possible without damaging the quality of storytelling. This book seeks ultimately to offer a general compilation of the myriad of interesting tales, historical records, anecdotes, and legends that form the canon of mischief in Trinity College in a fashion that is accessible and easily navigable to the history scholar and casual reader alike.

So enjoy this never-before-seen history of Trinity that strips back the veneer of order and shows the chaos that rests at the heart of Ireland's greatest university.

ONE

THE BIRTH OF
A UNIVERSITY
AND OF PRANKERY

In 1592, Trinity was established to provide a centre of learning for the members of the new Protestant gentry of Ireland. Protestantism was still moderately young at that time, and by no means solidified within England's dominions, and Queen Elizabeth was dedicated to the cause of creating an educated, loyal professional class across her realm. Conceived as the 'mother of a university', Trinity was meant to be the first of many constituent colleges in a broader University of Dublin, as was the case with the universities of Cambridge and Oxford. It began as a small square of red-brick buildings, one example of which remains today in the form of the Rubrics dormitory.

Trinity remained a very small institution for much of its first century of existence. This was not the fault of the College administration, but was rather the product of significant political instability during the period. Twice the College came under existential threat; first, when the central government collapsed in 1641 after the failed Irish uprising, which led to the vicious suppression under Cromwell, and second, when the brief Jacobite government of 1689 closed the

The Rubrics, the oldest remaining building in College. The Rubrics was constructed during the turmoil of the later seventeenth century and was completed around 1700. It remains a residence house for students and academic staff. (Aifric Ní Chríodáin)

Oliver Cromwell. After overthrowing Charles I of England, Cromwell led a war in Ireland against royalist forces that ran the risk of destroying the young Trinity College. (Wikimedia Commons)

College and expelled all the students and Fellows. Fortunately for the future of Trinity, the library was spared in both these upheavals and remained the nucleus for the university moving forward.

The extent and extremity of the political crisis in Ireland throughout the seventeenth century has left little information on typical student life outside what is recorded in the dry history texts. What little is known of the early days, such as they were, are recorded somewhat anecdotally much later on. What is known is that what passed for pranks and mischief was of a much darker sort than would today be considered the norm, no doubt due to the darker and more lawless times in which the early students lived.

Revenge

One account of an early prank involved two students setting upon a path of revenge against a Fellow of the College who had marked them harshly in their exams. They contrived to send the lecturer a false summons into the city, pretending to have important business with him. Disguising themselves as coalporters, the two students waited for the Fellow to pass by them in the street and set upon him from behind, shouting and sputtering that the Fellow had been carousing with one of their wives. After roughing the man up they made good their escape. Following the incident, the poor academic did not leave the grounds of the College for some years.

Rustication

A term that deserves mentioning, and which came into the common parlance during this early period of the University, and that would find ample use in the hands of its disciplinarians for over two centuries, is the concept of rustication. Were a student to step too far out of line, he would be sent back down to the country, and thus rusticated. The fear of such punishment was one of the only things that could keep the boisterous students in line, but oftentimes it would prove still not enough.

While stories and evidence of pranks and mischief from this early period are scant on the ground, it was because of the chaos that the next century, in which order was restored in practical terms yet in which the spirit of lawlessness remained, would become a fertile ground for pranks never again rivalled.

TWO

THE GOLDEN AGE OF MAYHEM: TRINITY IN THE EIGHTEENTH CENTURY

After a prolonged succession dispute in England, culminating in the Jacobite Rebellion and the Battle of the Boyne, Irish society was severely divided in the early eighteenth century; a state of affairs that would continue with varying severity for decades. This division was acutely visible inside the walls of Trinity College. The sons of Jacobites made up a large proportion of the student body and were angry and noisome students who proved an unruly lot, especially when set against the more staunchly loyalist of their fellow students. Worse still, the College administration, led by the austere and stern Provost Richard Baldwin, represented a bulwark of loyalist opinion. The unfortunate result was that a large number of students came to hold the authorities of the College in contempt. Anarchy truly reigned in the halls, even as it had been restored to the streets of Dublin with the reassertion of English political dominion.

The disorder was increased yet further by apathy amongst the general College academic staff. Peter Boyle, in a paper on the life and times of Provost Baldwin, describes the attitude of the teaching staff in ungenerous terms: 'We are told that

James II. Deposed by Protestant influences in the 1688 Glorious Revolution, James still found many loyal followers in Ireland. The Catholic, Jacobite government of 1689 briefly disbanded the Protestant Trinity College. (Wikimedia Commons)

the lecturers didn't lecture, and that the Fellows neither prayed in Chapel nor dined in Hall'. Yet it was largely thanks to this political conflict and administrative neglect that this period became the golden age of pranks and mischief in Trinity College.

The Junior Dean

One major example of student mischief in this period involved the Junior Dean, who was tasked with responsibility for discipline and perennial enemy of student fun, publicly reprimanding a student for poor behaviour. Conventionally, a student so chastened would flee to his room to lick his wounds after a harsh scolding, but this time things went very differently. Enraged at the Dean's words, the student and his friends proceeded to hurl stones and other heavy objects at the poor administrator. The Junior Dean fled the scene, but the students were not done. Gathering friends, they stormed off to the main entrance of the College where they attempted to burn the front gate down. Angered at the students' outrageous behaviour, the Board publicly offered a reward for any information about who had led the arson attempt. No one was forthcoming, as several students offered their own higher reward for the hides of anyone who talked to the Board.

Young Bucks

The students of this era did not make the College the only site of their mayhem. Jonathan Bardon, in his *A History of Ireland in 250 Episodes*, describes the general behaviour of the rowdy Trinity student thus:

> Sons of nobles and gentlemen for the most part, they strode about wearing gowns trimmed with gold or silver according to rank. Some could afford to dine at the Eagle Tavern, home of the notorious Hell-Fire Club, or risk a duel at Lucas's Coffee-House on Cork Hill.
>
> Others would eat beefsteaks in The Old Sot's Hole on Essex Bridge or mingle with the humbler classes in the ale-houses of Winetavern Street. Generally known as 'bucks', they were often eager to join fights in the narrow streets, wielding the heavy keys to their rooms as weapons.

These young bucks made a habit of mischief and trouble for which the College became famous. Those sons of gentlemen who wore special braiding on their robes to mark them out from the common students were the worst of the lot and were true terrors outside of Trinity's walls. Turning their hats and robes inside out to evade easy identification, they threw stones at passers-by from their carriages as they rode through the streets of Dublin.

A Riot at the Smock Alley Theatre

The students of Trinity often came into direct conflict with the city authorities as a result of their obscene behaviour. On one occasion, in 1747, a student of Trinity found himself at odds with Thomas Sheridan, the manager of the Smock Alley Theatre, an establishment that hosted many of Ireland's great playwrights of the era, when he was refused admission backstage. The custom of the time in such theatres was for members of the public to be able to pay for the privilege of going backstage to meet and hobnob with the actors, a practice that Sheridan had recently dispensed with. Upon hearing that he would not be admitted, the student, who was severely inebriated at the time, proceeded to lead a group of his friends in tearing up the theatre.

Abduction of the Bailiff

On another occasion, again in 1747, a student who had run up a number of bills in the city found himself arrested on campus and removed to languish in jail. The students of the College, aroused to anger by what they considered to be an unjustified imprisonment, took to the streets and began a rampage. They started by abducting the bailiff who had arrested their friend and brought him back to College, where they proceeded to hold his head under the communal water pump, nearly drowning the man (this treatment was apparently a popular one among students for punishing their peers who had transgressed for various reasons). Not satisfied with kidnapping, the student mob continued in their ruckus with a violent and fiery riot in the city, culminating in the storming of the jail where their fellow student was held. Provost Baldwin was hard pressed to deal with the situation.

Richard Baldwin. As Trinity's longest serving Provost, Baldwin helped shape the College into its modern form. More than willing to get his hands dirty when occasion demanded, Baldwin earned the respect of his young charges. (Liam Brophy)

Harried by the city fathers and constabulary, the Provost was not able to exact much justice from his young charges. A number of students were reprimanded, amongst them a young Oliver Goldsmith who would go on to be one of Ireland's great poets and playwrights.

While a strict man, Provost Baldwin did not always face off against the riotous students for whom he was responsible. As Peter Boyle recounted in a presentation on the life of Baldwin, the Provost defended a number of students against the deputies of the Lord Mayor who demanded their arrest after a particularly nasty fight between the young gentlemen of the College and some workmen of the city.

The Provost refused the Mayor's demand, claiming that the students must surely have been provoked by some insult, and sent the despondent city official reeling back to the city hall. Baldwin's defence of the students led some of them to commission a portrait of the Provost in gratitude, one that hangs in the College still today.

Trinity Students Versus Dublin Gangs

Conflicts between Trinity students and Dublin gangs were also rife in this period of lawlessness. The streets of Dublin were crowded with groups of thugs, mostly consisting of younger members of the various trade guilds. The most famous gang conflict during this era was the result of a lengthy feud; on one side stood the Butchers, and on the other were the Tailors and the Weavers, who were known collectively as the Liberty Boys. The Butchers in particular were known for their brutality, and it was said that they hung their captured enemies by their jaws on hooks in their meat lockers. Boyle describes pitched battles in the streets, in which 'up to 1,000 men sometimes engaged in vicious street fighting that could last the whole day'. Many foolhardy Trinity bucks sought out these groups and took ample part in their brutal combats. After one particularly nasty confrontation with the Butchers, a few Trinity students were captured and carried off to the meat locker.

Fearing their fellow students would suffer a terrible fate at the Butchers' hands, a group set out from College on a rescue mission. They found their friends had been spared a grisly fate, and had merely been hung on the hooks by their belts.

These gang fights were common and could break out at almost any time. A procession of students heading to St Patrick's Cathedral during the Lenten season was attacked by a gang of Butchers. Provost Baldwin was amongst the throng of students, and the young men, upon seeing the danger, closed ranks to defend their leader. But the Provost would not be held back when the students under his charge were in danger and strode to the front of the procession. A man of prodigious bravery, Baldwin is reported to have shouted, 'Follow me, my lads, and I'll head you, and I'll fight for you till I die', before charging into the fray. The Provost's fury was enough to send the Butchers reeling, and Trinity won the day. A student who witnessed Baldwin's leadership that day described him as being 'brave as a lion'. Courageous he must have been, as few academics would likely be said to be able to hold their own against an angry gang and to lead an army of students into battle.

No doubt the chaotic days of the eighteenth century are long behind Trinity, which has since settled into the scholarly and introspective atmosphere expected of most great universities. Yet even though the College is no doubt a more refined place of learning in the absence of bucks and gangs and

Baldwin's Memorial. Set in the Exam Hall, Baldwin's memorial dominates the room, just as the man dominated the College in life. (Liam Brophy)

street riots, it is surely a less exciting place. It is certainly hard to imagine any of today's lecturers, let alone the Provost, fighting valiantly in the streets of Dublin, and it really is a pity. So here's to the spirit, if not the deeds, of Old Trinity.

THREE

GUNS, GHOSTS AND TALL TALES

The Murder of Edward Ford

In over 400 years of its history, Trinity has been host to many acts of violence and vandalism. In 1663, for example, a Fellow of the College by the name of Leckey was executed for treason for plotting against the King. Yet only once in its long history has Trinity been witness to a deliberate act of murder, albeit one that began as a prank.

Edward Ford was one of Trinity's brightest up-and-coming academics. As a student he was named a Foundation Scholar, an honour only afforded to the most gifted students after passing a gruelling set of examinations during their second year as undergraduates. He followed up his undergraduate studies with receipt of an MA, and was elected a Junior Fellow of the College in 1730, at the age of twenty-four.

However, despite his academic prowess, Ford was not a popular man. He quickly developed a reputation as a harsh disciplinarian who meddled often in the affairs of students, admonishing them for tardiness, drunkenness and other rule-breaking. On one occasion, Ford sought to investigate the vandalizing of a colleague's rooms, and confronted certain students. For these efforts Ford received a number of anonymous threatening letters. The students of the College came to despise Ford, and he became the object of much ridicule among the undergraduates who immensely disliked his frequent disruptions to their revelries. Ford's unpopularity with the student body would eventually boil over into a conflict that would become one of Trinity's most oft-told tales.

Late on the night of 7 March 1734, a small group of students coming home after a night of heavy drinking and carousing around the city, were accosted by one of the College porters at the Front Gate. It is unclear why, perhaps fuelled by the strong drink, but the students attacked the porter and beat him quite severely. Making their way across the Front Square towards their apartments, the gang was confronted by Ford who had been drawn by the sound of the commotion. Ford admonished the young men for their dissolute and disgraceful behaviour, haranguing them back to their apartments.

The students, however, had no plans of going to bed. Enraged by the abuse they had received from the hated lecturer, the students reconvened in one of the residential common rooms and there set upon a plan of revenge. They gathered outside Ford's apartment, which was located on the first floor of the Rubrics, the College's oldest building that housed much of the academic staff. The drunken students threw stones at Ford's window, breaking several panes. Drawn out by the commotion, Ford stood amid the shattered glass and shouted down at the rowdy group. Enraged, the young lecturer drew out the black-powder pistol he kept at his bedside and fired it at his rock-wielding assailants, grazing one of them. The students scattered at the sound of gunfire and fled back to their apartments once more.

Parliament Square, now called Front Square, is the most
iconic section of Trinity College and the setting of many of the
most memorable pranks. (Aifric Ní Chríodáin)

However, a number of the students were still not chastened
and happened to be in possession of pistols. A group of them
gathered up their firearms and set off back to the Rubrics,
ready for battle. Shouting at Ford to come and face them and
hurling more debris at his window, they goaded their enemy to
come out to his window. Ignoring the advice of a student on his
floor to ignore the interlopers, Ford returned to the window
clad in his nightgown to answer their challenge. The students
outside proceeded to fire upon their much maligned lecturer,
striking him in the chest. Seeing that they had hit their quarry,
the drunken marauders scattered.

Upon hearing the gunshots, a number of students rushed
up to find Ford lying in a pool of blood and broken glass. Ford
asked them to bring a surgeon. Realizing the man was dying, they
quickly called the College authorities who came to attend to
the stricken lecturer. When the surgeon arrived he attempted to

bleed the dying man, hardly useful for a man rapidly succumbing to blood loss. His last words were attributed be a wish that God forgive the students who had shot him.

The furore that arose from the slaying was immediate and intense. The porters were called out in force, and the police were brought into College. The students and staff who had been nearest the scene of the crime made accusations against certain students, and the investigators set out in pursuit. At the same time as the incident, a party was being held at the far end of the Rubrics, at which a number of students were found to be clinging to a punchbowl full of a brew toxic with alcohol. In the room the investigators also found powder and a pistol that had been fired recently. Some of these young men were named as the culprits in the foul murder. Several students were expelled. But the legal battle was yet to come.

Five students were put on trial for the murder. History records their names as Cotter, Crosby, Scholes, Davis, and Boyle. In the run-up to the trial, a friend of the accused, named Benjamin Barrington, spent a great deal of time seeking out students of the College who could be prevailed upon to offer false affidavits in support of their fellow students. During the trial, many witnesses were called. The porter, the only real eyewitness to the men who had first been admonished by Ford, and who had received a beating from them, was unable to identify any of the accused as the culprits, as he too had been under the influence of alcohol that night and thus had little recollection of what had transpired. Other witnesses included students and staff living in and near the Rubrics, but again their testimonies proved unhelpful to the prosecution, as they were often contradictory and predominantly circumstantial. Ultimately the judge moved the jury to acquit on two bases: first, due to the lack of concrete evidence, and second, that the whole affair was little more than

Number 25. This house, still used to accommodate students and staff, was the sight of the shooting of Edward Ford. (Aifric Ní Chríodáin)

a student prank that had gotten out of hand. It is hard to imagine such leniency being shown to such 'pranksters' today!

In the end, the murderers escaped justice. But the story did not end there. In fact, several of those accused went on to lead very successful lives. Cotter would go on to be elected an MP, and was later named a baronet. Crosby eventually became a viscount and was later created an earl. Benjamin Barrington, for all his questionable legal dealing, found great success in the Church, eventually rising to be Dean of Armagh Cathedral.

In the immediate aftermath of the whole affair, rather than being praised for his decision to expel suspected murderers from the College, the Provost was denounced by the parents of many students for his mistreatment of 'the sons of gentlemen', and that he had taken action over what was no more than a 'frolick'. The College authorities were further besieged by complaints from the Dublin city government, who were incensed at the incident. Only months before the fateful incident the College had assured the police that the policy prohibiting the possession of firearms on the College grounds was strictly enforced. The murder of Edward Ford proved this statement to the contrary, much to the embarrassment of the College.

The legend of Edward Ford has developed something of a life of its own after so many retellings, and there have even been occasional reports over the years of the slain man's ghost stalking the area around Rubrics. These sightings have been recorded many times. Professor C. Maxwell, in *A History of Trinity College Dublin*, describes a report of such a spectral visitation:

> … his ghost, dressed in wig, gown and knee breeches, is said to walk by the side of the Rubrics at dusk … he emerges slowly from the door of his old chambers at number 25, walks more briskly in the direction of Botany Bay, and then fades into darkness.

Other spectral sightings have included sightings of 'a confused and shadowy mob' appearing outside the Rubrics, no doubt poor Ford's assailants coming to mock and torment him even in death.

Another legend has sprung up around Edward Ford, having to do with one of the oldest societies in the College, the University Philosophical Society, known around Trinity as the Phil. The Society's elders claim that the men who shot Ford were members of the Phil's governing council, and that the incident resulted in the Society's expulsion from the College for more than a century. This story is told to all incoming freshmen who become involved in the Society, and is given the weight of full historic solemnity. However, the story is a complete fabrication, as the Phil was not founded until 1843, a century after Ford's untimely end. This tall tale may be one of the most oft-repeated fallacies about Trinity's history, making its creators and propagators some of the most successful pranksters of the College.

FOUR

A PRANKSTER'S GUIDE TO TRINITY COLLEGE

In 1791 a mysterious volume began to be sold by the bookshops and vendors of Dublin. Entitled *Advice to the University of Dublin*, the book was a comprehensive set of guidelines to all members of Trinity College on how best to abuse their various positions in the academic and social hierarchy. A section was dedicated to each of the high officials, and also to each of the student groupings, from freshman to rising bachelors. The book was an immediate hit among the students and reviled by the academic staff who saw it as promoting loose morals and flaunting and making light of their authority. Copies made the rounds of the College like wildfire, and were common reading for many years. Authorship of the text remains unknown, but it appears to be the work of an elder student or recent graduate. No doubt he hid his identity in order to avoid the hefty punishment promised by the academics so thoroughly lampooned within its pages.

General Advice for Students

While *Advice* addresses all students and staff in their various roles, its real charm is found in its advice to the students of the College, in how best to make mischief and circumvent the

Byzantine rules of the Provost and Junior Dean. It advises new students to 'take out rooms in the College, for this reason that you will have an opportunity of playing many pranks, which you could not in a lodging in town'. Such 'pleasant frolics' were to include the throwing of loud firecrackers from windows late at night in order to startle and frighten the Fellows who had taken early to bed. It also recommends a life of heavy drinking, fighting and carousing as the best means for boys to become men and to be 'initiated into the several mysteries of Bacchus, Venus, and Mars'.

To the wider body of students, *Advice* gives further instruction. During exams students were to cut the tassels off of the academic gowns of those around them paying too close attention to the subject at hand. They are advised also to carve their names and whatever obscenities came to mind into the surface of their desks in order to inform future generations of students of their daring and lack of care for all things studious. Anyone who has seen the graffiti etched onto the desks in today's lecture theatres will recognise that this advice has continued to be well regarded by present undergraduates more than 200 years on.

The Importance of Not Studying

The one activity *Advice* is disgusted by and absolutely adamant that no student should ever engage in is the act of actually studying. Young men of a studious disposition were to be reviled beyond all other criminals. It was every student's duty to make sure that no one else engaged upon such a scholarly path, for it was not enough that one merely not study, but that no student be trapped by the cruel fate of the bookworm or library rat. Reading, surely, was something done by other people, not virile young men who had much more pressing matters at hand, such as drinking, fighting, and pranking. *Advice* gives several suggestions on how to rescue other lads from their studies. Among these was to raise an enormous racket every time one returned to one's rooms, thus breaking all currently indoors from their concentration and arousing them to the possible pleasures to be had outside their cloistered dormitories. If such noise making was insufficient to arouse one's fellows, students were to knock on scholars' doors and give the illusion of being porters.

When the unwary studier opened his door, one was to burst in and make a mess of the lad's room so as to make further study impossible. If even this effort failed, one could use a hot poker from the fire to bore holes through the roof or floor of a student's room to cause persistent annoyance from above and below.

Other potential pranks involved a degree of theft and defacement:

> You will shortly be esteemed a man of humour if you accustom yourself to playing tricks on the porters and badgmen; to carry away unperceived from the rooms of your acquaintances, a gown, book, &c., and to return them again with a laugh, after keeping the owners in pain, searching for them; to write with chalk or charcoal, bawdy words on the most obvious parts of the walls; to scratch out the names that are on the doors of the various chambers, or certain letters of a name, so as to convert the remainder into some laughable word.

These types of pranks have made their way into the modern arsenal of pranksters not only in Trinity, but in schools and universities around the world.

Avoiding Chapel

A constant annoyance to the students of the College, from its foundation well into the nineteenth century, was the perpetuation of rules mandating attendance at chapel services several times a week. Being forced to rise early in the morning, particularly on Sundays after long nights on the town, was especially irksome to many. *Advice* suggests that a way around this might be to feign illness and thus to take meals and other services in one's rooms. Students could also use the time spent during services to preen for young ladies in the galleries and to carve their names into the pews for posterity.

Improving Finances

Advice also has a lot to say about that perpetual bane of students: money. Students in the eighteenth century were as short on funds as their contemporary counterparts, though they had significantly cleverer and cheekier ways of getting around the limitations of their budgets. Students are advised to take out long lines of credit with public houses and other purveyors of goods, and told to dodge repayment wherever possible, either by frequently changing their venues of revelry, or using false names to avoid the debt collectors. For the sons of gentlemen, *Advice* suggests they do everything they can to increase their allowances from their fathers, such as inflating the apparent costs of food, clothes, books, etc. The rationale for all this is of course that the more spending money you have, the more you can expend on drink and dissolution. Another financial gambit *Advice* suggests is to develop a rapport with one of the lecturers or professors in order to get them to develop a line of credit with the College larder. After doing so, it then became possible to thieve one of the lecturer's credit books and to forge his signature. In so doing one could significantly increase one's income of goods at the College's expense.

Duelling and Street Fighting

Matters of honour and bravery were major preoccupations of students of the seventeenth and eighteenth centuries in Trinity, and the subject of duelling is discussed in some detail in *Advice*. A club for the express purpose of instructing young gentlemen in the art of swordplay had already been founded some years before the publication of *Advice*, and it seems that matters of honour were often decided by this means by students, even though such fights were against both the rules of College and the laws of the city. *Advice* recognises that discretion is often the better part of valour, and gives a great deal of time to the ways by which students might save face without fear of injury by pistol or blade. It suggests that students who were so affronted by another's behaviour as to be required to demand satisfaction, should challenge his opponent to a duel at a set time and place and then inform the bailiffs of the same so that they may break up the dispute before violence could ensue. If challenged likewise, students should make such a public pronouncement of their lack of fear and eagerness to fight that it would come to the College administration's attention and be similarly broken up before it began. By such careful manoeuvring, a young gentleman of Trinity could build a fearsome reputation as a warrior and man of honour while never once actually coming into harm's way. Similar suggestions are given with regard to the various street fights that were frequent occurrences in the latter part of the eighteenth and early nineteenth century.

Advice cautions those students lacking in physical strength but possessing in speed and guile on how best to develop a fearsome reputation as a street scrapper. By sneaking up behind one's opponents and striking quickly before retreating behind a wall of one's larger friends, a smaller student could still be counted amongst the victorious number at battle's end.

The Consequences of Mischief

Advice acknowledges the fact that if a student takes its suggestions to heart they will no doubt face the College's discipline at some stage. No matter how clever or careful you are in your mischief making, you will eventually get caught. When this happened, students usually faced fines and other pecuniary penalties, or were forced to do extensive writing drills as punishments, usually involving complex translations into Latin. In the instance of financial penalties, *Advice* is fairly flippant, declaring that the sums are usually fairly petty and should thus be taken as further reason for students to hold the rules of the College in contempt. In the case of translation drills, it encourages students to make use of them in such a way as to turn the tables on the disciplinarians, by recording as ribald and mocking a translation as possible.

Sometimes, however, the punishment could be more severe. If a student was faced with suspension, or rustication, he was expected to leave the city and return to the countryside in disgrace until such time as the College deemed him fit to return to its more polite company. Yet the crueller elements of this punishment could be avoided if one were possessed of caution and guile. *Advice* suggests that students suffering from rustication take up lodgings elsewhere in the city, off the beaten path of the Fellows, and thus have full access to the night life of Dublin, absent the various responsibilities of student life.

Advice for Graduates

Advice also reaches beyond the student life and offers some instruction to those young men about to graduate and seek their fortunes outside the hallowed halls of Trinity. If students had taken its guidance so far, they would be fairly under-qualified in any academic sense, so the range of options would be scant indeed. *Advice* recommends to the young men with some savings to seek a career in law or at least to go on to one of the Inns of Court in London to ostensibly study the law for a few years. Doing so would allow them to continue the same ribald lives to which they had become accustomed for some years further. For those without such fortunes, a career in the Church is suggested. Such a path would, *Advice* insists, 'serve as asylum for past, and a sanction of future iniquity'.

One of the Inns of Court, the Honourable Society of the King's Inns was and is Ireland's premier barrister school. *Advice* suggests that continuing one's education in such an institution could prolong one's fun and games for several years after graduating from Trinity. (Trinity Foundation)

Advice certainly had some impact on the students of Trinity, and thus on the administration whose duty it was to govern them. In many ways the book was merely recording and codifying practices that had been in full and regular use for a century or more, but its easy accessibility expanded the number of mischief-makers considerably. The true impact of the book thus cannot be fully ascertained, but it remains a major window into life on the ground in Trinity during the more lawless days of centuries' past.

FIVE

POLITICAL MISCHIEF

Trinity students have long been keen followers of politics, but it was at the end of the eighteenth and dawn of the nineteenth century during which they held greatest sway and interest in

Irish Parliament House. Right across the street from Trinity, the Irish Parliament had a close relationship with the students of the College. Today the building is used as the headquarters of the Bank of Ireland. (Aifric Ní Chríodáin)

the highest affairs of state. This period certainly marked the high point of direct influence on politics students of Trinity were ever to possess.

The Students' Gallery

Up until the 1790s there was even a special balcony in the Irish Parliament, then located just across the street from the College in what is now the Bank of Ireland building, reserved specifically for the gentlemen of Trinity to observe the proceedings. The balcony was set directly behind the Speaker's chair and thus afforded an excellent view of the debates as they unfolded on the floor of the House. Students made frequent use of this privilege, often well past the point of abuse, as J.E. Walsh points out in his short work, *Ireland Ninety Years Ago*:

> The student's passport was his gown ... This was a privilege often abused. The students' gowns were lent out indiscriminately to friends and acquaintances, and the gallery appeared sometimes half full of gownsmen, not half of whom were members of the University.

This privilege was eventually forfeited, however, when the students became unwilling to be mere passive witnesses to the affairs of state. In 1795, Lord Fitzwilliam, the Viceroy, was recalled to London after overstepping his remit by offering greater political independence to Irish Catholics than the government in Westminster was willing to allow. When the subject of the Viceroy's sudden departure came up for debate in the House, the gallery was packed with excited students. Henry Grattan, one of the most distinguished orators ever produced by Trinity College, led a fiery denunciation of the

Grattan Monument. Henry Grattan was one of the greatest orators in Irish political history. A graduate of Trinity, his monument stands on College Green between Trinity College and the old Irish Parliament. (Aifric Ní Chríodáin)

government, claiming it had offered promises of reform in the guise of Lord Fitzwilliam, only to jerk them away at the last moment. At the height of Grattan's speech the students could no longer suppress their enthusiasm for the words of that generation's Demosthenes, and burst forth in loud and lengthy applause and calls of support, for political and legal reform was a cherished issue among the youths of Trinity. The disturbance was so great that the Speaker ordered the gallery cleared. That scene resulted in the permanent revocation of attendance privileges, as the Speaker 'had counted on the loyalty and propriety of the students of the University, and this display of what he considered riot and sedition at once changed his estimate of their character'.

The students thereafter begged the Speaker for a restoration of their rights, going so far to petition him at his office on an almost daily basis, but it all proved to be of no avail.

The Historical Society

Merely watching the parliamentary debates was already insufficient political sport to sate the burgeoning civic appetites of the students. They wanted to participate in a more active manner. They found such an opportunity in the shape of the Historical Society, the debating club established in 1770 for the further education of members of the College in the art of oratory. The Society was governed strictly by the College Board, which demanded the right to review all motions and resolutions put forward to the members for debate. This preoccupation by the administration toward the Society was furthered in the wake of the two abortive rebellions, of 1798 and 1803, led by Theobald Wolfe Tone and Robert Emmet respectively. Both men had been active members

Theobald Wolfe Tone was an active member of the College Historical Society while a student in Trinity. He would lead the unsuccessful 1798 rebellion, after which failure he took his own life while in prison. (Wikimedia Commons)

of the Historical Society while students in Trinity, and many other current and former members, participated in their failed uprisings. In the run-up to the 1798 uprising, the Board expelled a number of the Society's more firebrand members from College entirely. The Board insisted also that the Society not debate any issues of modern politics and to instead limit itself to debates on historical issues. The Society complied with this edict for a time, but finally pushed the Board too far when, in 1812, it proposed the question for debate, 'Was Brutus justifiable in putting Julius Caesar to death?'

While this debate was not technically a matter of modern politics, the Provost perceived it to be referring to their present-day circumstances and as a coded attack upon the right of English rule of Ireland. The eventual result of the tension between the Society and the Provost was the expulsion of the Society from College.

While members of the Society continued to meet outside of the College for many years, it would not return to Trinity until 1843, when the chilling effect on public discourse had abated somewhat with the fading of the memory of the uprisings at the turn of the century. Cut off from active participation in the wider political discourse by order of the College authorities, students would come to turn their attentions and energies during the nineteenth century once more toward their age-old enemies in the College hierarchy.

Robert Emmet, the leader of an unsuccessful rebellion against England in 1803, for which he was executed. Emmet had been a prominent student and political activist while studying at Trinity. (Wikimedia Commons)

SIX

BATTLE ON THE QUAD

George Salmon was one of the strictest and most conservative Provosts in the long history of Trinity College. A noted mathematician and theologian, Salmon made an academic career of battling the Catholic Church and what he believed to be papist heresies. Elected Provost in 1888, he brought the same crusading zeal with which he had fought popery to his new office, and for nearly two decades served as a bulwark against change, and was a fierce champion of tradition. One of his most famed stands against unseemly progress was his struggle for many years to prevent women from gaining admittance to the College, which he is alleged to have said would happen only 'over his dead body'. Time would prove this sentiment true, as in January 1904, days after Provost Salmon was laid to rest for the final time, the first women were admitted as students.

Provost Salmon was deeply concerned during his early years at Trinity's helm with what he considered to be a growing laxity of college discipline, particularly from undergraduate students. The chief reason for this degeneration of discipline was placed at the feet of Dr Thomas Thompson Gray, who had served as the Junior Dean, the chief disciplinarian, since 1877. Dr Gray was a friendly academic who had little interest in enacting excessive punishments upon his young charges. Generations of students come to realise that the good doctor would not seek to enforce many of the rules of the College, and had learned to get around the few rules Dr Gray had, as a matter of form, the compunction to attempt to enforce. Gray's carefree attitude was immortalised in a play, written in 1892 to commemorate the College's tercentenary. *Botany Bay: A Play in One Act* tells the story of students seeking to hold an illicit drinking party in their rooms, only to be caught out by the Junior Dean. Yet the good-natured Dr Gray allows the revels to continue, saying, 'I will forgive your hilarity this once on account of your desire to commemorate the tercentenary'. In truth, the students of Trinity had a very real fondness for their Junior Dean, a sentiment rarely held for such officials of the College. Dr Gray's likeability has never fully been matched since, and not even rivalled until the twentieth century, and the office of Junior Dean has, to the present day, generally been the most reviled by students.

Provost Salmon was set upon another path to mark the tercentenary in 1892, choosing to cap off the year with a reshuffle of administrative offices, including Dr Gray's. The Provost's plan was to appoint a new Junior Dean who shared his own strict attachment to the rules and discipline. He found his man in the form of Dr George Wilkins, a taciturn tyrant whose term as a master of Classics at the High School, one of Dublin's most prestigious and strictly administered schools, honed his skills as an enforcer of hard discipline. Dr Wilkins received his commission from the Provost on 20 November, and set about his task of reining in student lawlessness with gusto. Records show that the new Junior Dean took his first action mere hours after his appointment, catching a young undergraduate who had been making a wobbly attempt at a furtive entrance back into College after a lengthy night on the town. This fateful first crackdown would have far-reaching consequences for the Provost's new enforcer and the state of discipline in Trinity.

Upon hearing of their fellow student's plight at the hands of Dr Wilkins, the undergraduate residents of the College came out in forceful protest. That very night, students gathered in the residential square known as Botany Bay. There they lit bonfires and tended them through the night, and each time the fearsome Junior Dean, his deputies, or the College porters sought to disperse the mob, they were driven back with taunting abuse.

The denizens of Botany Bay had a long tradition of independence of spirit, and bonfires had been known to be lit from time to time all through the nineteenth century, with the last recorded ones being lit in the 1940s. It is unclear where the name Botany Bay arose for the residence quad, but many contended that it came from the Australian settlement, at which Irish convicts led a bloody uprising in 1801.

David Alfred Chart, in his 1907 *The Story of Dublin*, lent support to this view, saying it 'received its name from the prison-like style of its architecture and the supposed character of the undergraduates, who resort there as to an Alsatia out of the reach of the law'. Whether or not the square was named thusly, the students certainly gave their best effort to live up to their infamous namesake. For many years before and after that fateful November, the residents of Botany developed a rather frightful reputation for lawlessness.

George Wilkins, faced with such formidable and unexpected opposition from the residents, despaired at what to do. The bonfires lit the night he took office and began his ill-fated foray into Botany Bay, continued to burn for nearly a week with no sign of abating. At his wit's end, poor Dr Wilkins, thoroughly defeated by the defiance of the student body, sought swift exit from his

Botany Bay, one of the major dormitories in College, is still in use today. In 1892, Botany Bay was a vision of chaos, filled with bonfires and uncontrollable to the Junior Dean and his deputies. (Aifric Ní Chríodáin)

plight. He met with the Board of the College on 26 November, which had only just confirmed his appointment scant days before, and submitted his resignation. The Board, however, refused to accept it, insisting that Wilkins do his duty and break up the rioting mob.

Unwilling to suffer any further indignities at the hands of the vicious youths, poor Wilkins entreated Provost Salmon to relieve him of his duties. The Provost, upset at the sudden outbreak of chaos, relieved Wilkins and began a frantic search for someone who might be able to put an end to the madness in Botany Bay. He found Alexander Charles O'Sullivan, a young and well-liked lecturer known in College as Tully, willing to take up the onerous task of restoring order. Tully was a highly energetic man, and had been a keen rower and golfer when a student in Trinity. He would later distinguish himself during the First World War as a field surgeon, showing the same mettle on the battlefield as he displayed during his brief time as Trinity's chief of discipline.

Appointed Acting Junior Dean hours after Wilkins' resignation, Tully quickly set about breaking up the disturbance in Botany Bay. He found a number of able lieutenants, first among them Anthony Traill, a tough lecturer who had previously served as High Sheriff of Antrim, and who would later be named Provost Salmon's successor. Accompanied by a contingent of porters, some of the more spry Fellows and a few students still loyal to the College authorities, Tully marched upon the centre of Botany Bay, where the bonfires still blazed.

Rounding up the supposed ringleaders, and other major agents of disruption, Tully managed to physically expel a small mob of students from the College grounds. Tully and his confederates went so far as to raid a number of the common rooms in the residence hall and to turf out participants in the recent fray who had sought shelter indoors. Many students did not go quietly, and a number of Tully's men found themselves bruised and

George Salmon. Provost Salmon sought to bring a new level of order to Trinity in 1892, only to have his new Junior Dean outmatched by the angry mob of undergraduates. This incident did not, however, prevent a monument being erected to his memory in Front Square. (Aifric Ní Chríodáin)

battered from resistance. Tully himself was tackled roughly to the ground at the height of the conflict by Brian O'Brien, who was at the time a leading member of the University Football Club and would go on to play Rugby for Ireland a number of times in the 1890s. But in the end, Tully and his men prevailed over the rabble of students, the fires were extinguished, and order restored.

The great battle in Botany Bay was immortalised in verse form, possibly by Justice Gerald Fitzgibbon, who had family members at Trinity at the time. The poem, composed originally in Latin, is written as a parody of Virgil's *Aeneid*, with meter and verse corresponding closely to Book II of that work, which describes the Fall of Troy. The poem never saw the light of day until it was discovered in the Fitzgibbon Family Papers many years after the events it describes. The poem was printed in the 1958 edition of *Trinity: An Annual Record*, under the title 'Battle in Botany Bay'. The following is the poem translated into English:

Arms and the man I sing, who lately came
From High School to the groves of Academe
And hoped to lead his life in honour here.
But Fate, the Fate of Colleges, forbade
That such a man hold sway in such a place.
So many are the colleges of youth.
One shines in this, another shines in that;
A third outstrips them both in learned zeal.
But one was founded by Eblana's Queen,
To one she granted statutes and a name,
And held it deep within her gloried heart.
And Salmon was its Provost. He decreed
That Gray renounce the keys, and in his place
The College elders named another Dean –
A Dean whose dearest care ye now shall learn.

For he, unschooled to emulate Gray's arts,
Began at once to crack too fierce a whip.
His first night out, he hauled before the law
A student he had collared, wracked with wine.
This was the source of riot most extreme:
Young men in togas raged, and now there rose
The wail of trumpets mixed with fighting cries.
Through the broad streets they rave; each pathway seethes.
The youths press on. They snatch up all the bins,
Set them alight, and revel in the blaze.
They hurl dry wood and tree trunks on the pyre,
They add the Muses' doors, and now the Bay
From end to end gleams with reflected flame.
But here, in front of all, there galloped in,
Flanked with a mighty throng of skips and porters,
This novice Dean. Through rod and flame he charged,
Where raging arms and rising clamour called.
At length, young allies lined up by his side.
Small Fry, then Tully comes, then Tony Traill
(That artful driver of the flying ball);
Whom when he saw resolved to take the field,
The Dean began to chide in strident words:
'Buck up, you men! What sloth so long detains ye?
The jibs are bearing all in flames away,
And you in lofty council lingered on
Till now?' At once, before these low-born words
Received reply, the battle was engaged.
Elusive students strove in mocking flight.
As Tully chased one down, his foot gave way.
He landed on his head. But as he rose,
The man himself could not suppress a smile.

Tully fulfilled the duties of Junior Dean for a further two weeks, ensuring that no further flare-ups against College authority occurred. None did. It seemed the students were satisfied with having defeated the hated Wilkins and saw no need to lodge any further protest against the College establishment. No doubt they also feared the retribution of Tully, who, while good-natured, had shown himself to be a formidable foe, one few of the residents of Botany Bay considered worth fighting again.

With peace reigning once more in the College, Tully stepped down and the Provost appointed M.W.J. 'Matty' Fry to the position. Dr Fry proved a much more lasting Junior Dean, serving a full five-year term and experiencing no major upsets during his tenure. Indeed, he took heed, as did all future Junior Deans, that the students of Trinity College were a force to be reckoned with.

SEVEN

LADS OF THE BOAT CLUB

The Dublin University Boat Club is one of the oldest and most respected institutions in Trinity. Originally two competing organisations, the Boat Club and Rowing Club merged in 1898 to form the DUBC that has enjoyed a history of competitive excellence ever since. The Boat Club has long maintained a reputation for camaraderie and laddishness, maintained by the watchful eye of an extensive network of past members known as the 'Old Boys'. This has led to a long continuity of traditions, some of which have included holding various regatta and social functions each year, but most importantly a commitment to playful mischief. This mischief was best demonstrated during an incident in 1903, when a number of troublemakers were on the team. Chief among these were two young bucks by the names of Mick Leahy and Arthur McNeight.

After a punishing performance at the Henley Regatta, during which one of the oarsmen vomited uncontrollably due to the physical strain only to be revived by a strong brandy, the team was rather disheartened having failed to win much else but a side race. To lift their spirits, Andrew Jameson, an

Henley Cup. The regatta, shown here in the early 1900s, was, and indeed still is, a frequent destination of the Boat Club. (Wikimedia Commons)

ex-Trinity rower and director of the Bank of Ireland sent the team a full crate of Champagne. The bottles certainly did a lot to dull the senses, but they failed to dull the pain of the day.

Mick and Arthur came to a decision, after polishing off the last of the Champagne, to attempt a daring act of mischief against the people of Henley. They contrived to put out all the lights in the town's high street. They gathered up a crew of four further compatriots and set about their task under cover of night. The street lights were operated by gas jets and could be easily disabled provided one could reach the controls. In order to do so, Mick and Arthur had their accomplices hoist them up at each light to cut off the gas. They proceeded in this fashion all along the street, gradually plunging the whole of the high street into darkness, save for one last light. As Mick was lifted to cut off this last light, members of the Henley police hove into view. Not amused by the boat club's antics, the police drew their batons and charged. As they approached, Mick succeeded in dousing the last light, blanketing them in total darkness. Just as he did so, his friends holding him up lost their nerve and fled, dumping poor Mick unceremoniously to the ground.

Springing lithely to his feet, Mick proceeded to flee along with his friends. They tore across Henley with the policemen in hot pursuit, splitting up so as to avoid capture. Mick and Arthur stuck together and gave a merry chase to their pursuers, but finally found themselves cornered by a high wall. Arthur managed to scale it with a bound, but Mick could not cleanly clear the wall; while he did make it over the top in the end, he managed to lose the bottom of his pants thanks to an array of broken glass laced atop the wall.

Apart from the destruction of Mick's clothes, the boat club boys escaped retribution entirely. The police were unable to make an arrest and their little prank went unpunished for good.

EIGHT

OVER (AND UP) THE WALLS

Trinity has enjoyed a long tradition of night climbing. Intrepid students have, at one point or another, sought to scale all of the College's many noble structures under cover of darkness, breaking all rules of health and safety for the thrill of the climb.

Night climbing in Trinity has traditionally had an informal character, and has most usually taken the form of students seeking entry to the College after hours. For many years, into the twentieth century, there were strict curfews, and officials held nightly roll-calls to ensure that no students were in violation. (Today, students living on the campus can come and go at any time, but nonresidents are barred from entry after midnight.) However, this stricture has been taken by many students, seeking to continue their revels in town after the pubs and clubs have all closed, as more of a challenge than an impediment. Many inventive means of getting past the nightly roll have been devised over the years. One method involved climbing back inside College grounds after a night on the town, then putting on one's nightclothes and running down to the porters in a fabricated panic. The aim of this stratagem was to convince the porter that you had been in bed since well before the roll-call and had not been aroused when the time came to stand and be counted. Other students removed the bars from their windows so that they could climb out after the roll was completed, by use of ropes if necessary. Others simply utilized the age-old tactic of greasing the porters' palms from time to time. Today, the time-honoured skill of getting past the porters after hours is still practiced by students, some of whom have even mastered the art of bluffing their way in past the night porters by various means, including use of counterfeit key cards (usually hotel swipe keys), often hastily fabricated after a night on the town.

Other less sophisticated individuals have taken to the scaling of the College's walls in order to gain egress. This climb was never without dangers, as the walls and fences are high and topped with not-so-decorative spikes that could cause an inebriated student no end of grief. Such climbers were much more common in the years before CCTV was wired around Trinity. A popular blind spot to still be exploited through the

Another treacherous ledge ventured upon by daring students was that of the Exam Hall. (Aifric Ní Chríodáin)

1990s was near the railway station just off campus, where there were a number of firm footholds in the outer wall that could be exploited even while quite drunk. This location has since been wired with a camera and is grimly monitored.

Now there are very few such blind spots, and those who know them are hard-pressed to reveal them to their fellow undergrads. Only a few hardy souls can be found willing to attempt the high climb, for fear of a hard fall or a hard time from the security men.

Trinity Ball

By far the most popular time of year for attempted scaling of the College walls is the night of the Trinity Ball. The Ball, an annual late spring tradition since 1959, is the high point of the Trinity social calendar and is a rather swanky affair. Seven thousand students dressed in black-tie or fine dresses come along to enjoy what has become the largest private music party in Europe. The entire College is shut down the day of the Trinity Ball and dozens of private security guards are hired to ensure order.

Music acts from across Europe, and sometimes further afield, play on three improvised stages set up around the campus. The only problem with the Trinity Ball is the price. Ticket prices exceed 70 euros every year. Unsurprisingly, this is out of the price range for many impoverished students. Most of these poor young men and women console themselves by holding alternative, and distinctly less expensive, parties called counter-balls. Or they go out on the town. But some courageous individuals choose to take the more daring road and try to get into the Trinity Ball by stealth or guile. Popular methods involve hiding in various areas of the College not patrolled by security, including cupboards and the dank and treacherous tunnels under the College (which are, of course, officially off limits, but accessible by a few little-known paths). One oft-repeated and no doubt apocryphal story involves a student entering College early in the morning already in his black-tie and scaling one of the more leafy trees on the campus with a hope to evading being seen by the roving patrols. This enterprising lad, so the story goes, was spotted early in the day by members of the security detail who saw fit to leave him in his hiding place all through the day, only to throw him out minutes before the Ball was to begin. A sad finish to a brave effort, but it is a fate that has been shared by many students over the years.

Rather than hiding, many students have taken the more direct road of scaling the walls after the Ball had gotten into full swing. Such an attempt is more perilous than in other circumstances, as the security details are far more numerous and more vigilant than on normal nights. The added difficulty of making the already awkward climb encumbered by dinner dress further heightens the danger. Many first-hand accounts of these climbs exist, including one by William Watts, who was Provost of the College from 1981 to 1991. While serving in that office, Provost Watts bore witness to many attempts to enter the Trinity Ball by the back way. He gives one particularly amusing account in his memoir:

> On one occasion as we returned to the house a gatecrasher who had climbed into the stable yard was attempting to climb a second wall into the garden at the back of the house. He lost his footing and fell through the roof of our greenhouse with a resounding crash, then stood up and smashed his way out through the side … Apparently uninjured, he left the demolished greenhouse behind and climbed out to Nassau Street once more. I heard nothing more from him, nor ever discovered who he was, but surely God must extend his special protection to people like him.

Whoever that young man was, he holds the great honour of being the student to have caused the most disruption and chaos to a Provost's home and get away scot free.

Another account of breaking into the Trinity Ball is given by Richard Marsh, whose 1981 poem 'Over the Wall to the Trinity Ball', has been published in various places. The poem tells the tale of Marsh and his friends and their successful adventure into the 1978 Trinity Ball. The poem in full goes as follows:

> The weary old hand of the publican
> Waved toward the clock:
> 'Your glasses now, please, it's past time to leave.
> Come, boys and girls – amach.'
> Old Trinity grads and other fine lads
> And lasses of every degree
> Drank down their Guinness and Harp to the finish
> For someone had plans for a spree.
> Up then and spake the bold Limerick Rake
> With a leader-like look on his face.
> At the sound of his voice, all the hubbub and noise
> Came to a stop in that place.
> 'Right, boys, now you might know that this is the night
> Of the annual Trinity Ball.
> Which of you here has the courage to dare
> To follow me over the wall?'
> From hundreds of throats came the time-honoured boast
> In voices well liquored and hoarse:
> 'We all to the man are yours to command –
> If the girls will come with us, of course.'
> This visiting Yank went along on the prank,
> The soberest one of the lot,
> To record as a bard for those who were jarred

The valorous deeds of the plot.
We trouped out the door with the Rake at the fore
And stopped at TCD's front gate.
'Look there,' said young Tom, and he lifted his arm,
Forgetting his valuable freight.
Billy-O quickly bent to prevent the descent
Of the Jameson towards its destruction.
Unfortunately, so did Breeda McGee,
And their heads met without introduction.
Young lads with passes and evening-gowned lasses
Were lined up the length of the street.
'Those fellows are daft,' said Tom with a laugh,
'For the fruit that is stolen is sweet.'
The Rake raised his hand and said, 'Those who can stand ...'
For he saw that they were very few.
He continued, '... Will all carry those who can't crawl.
My God, what a sick looking Crew.'
The wobbly parade with the Rake in the lead
Straggled round to the rear of the school.
Just off Westland Row there were others also
At the wall. Said the Rake, 'I'm no fool.'
So we followed him round to Pearse Street and found,
As if it were destined by Fate,
A new building site that was closed for the night,
With a ladder beyond a locked gate.
Up over we went, every lady and gent,
Though the women wore long and short skirts.
'After you, girls,' said one of the churls.
The ladies said, 'Oh, you're such flirts.'
They put up the ladder, but what was the matter?
The ones at the top couldn't see.
And those on the ground couldn't hear any sound

But a splash — Paddy taking a pee.
Then someone said, 'Shhh,' halting Pat in mid-stream,
And whispered, 'There's wardens around.'
The Rake took command and said, 'I've a plan.
Come all of ye down to the ground.'
Down they all got. We set off at a trot
With the ladder back over the gate.
When all had climbed over, what did I discover?
I'm holding the ladder! Hey, wait!
Now I who was brought just to watch, as I thought,
Find myself at the head of the charge.
Says the Rake, 'Have no fear.' But he's at the rear
Of a mad Irish mob that is large.
So I run with no choice down the street till a voice
Hollers, 'Left when you come to the lane.'
I'm running like hell and grateful the yell
Is drowned by an overhead train.
Round the corner we speed with myself in the lead,
Hoping to find no police.
But what's that ahead? I wonder with dread,
For I'm surely disturbing the peace.
'Sure 'tis only a lad and his girlfriend, bedad,
Trying to climb up the wall.
To the rescue,' I shout, and the words that come out
Sound Irish, not Yankee at all.
'Yer man, like, you know,' I say, trying to show
I belong with the rest of the boys.
The Limerick Rake whispers, 'For Jaysus' sake,
The divil take all of this noise.
'Up with the ladder and down with the chatter.
The invasion is set to begin.
Now over the top, and nobody stop,

Till this whole sickly Crew is within.'
The climb wasn't hard, but Seamus was jarred,
And couldn't find one of his shoes.
On his hands and his knees he went fast as you please.
He knew he had no time to lose.
Pretty Peggy was next, the flower of her sex,
Resplendent in evening array.
She climbed even quicker, afraid that her knickers
Would show – it was dark, anyway.
The last one was me, for I wanted to see
If any policemen would come.
And just when I got myself safe to the top,
I heard someone thoughtfully hum.
A man and a lad, both officially clad,
Stood squinting up into the dark.
Said the one to his mate, 'I think we're too late
To witness the boys on a lark.
'Never let it be thought that the Gardaí were caught
Unaware, it would damage our honour.
Enough of this natter. Take down the ladder.
Victory to the Garda Siochána!'
Back in Verse Number 8, we left with headaches
Billy-O and sweet Breeda McGee.
They've been off on their own for the rest of the poem,
Nursing their lumps over tea.
But now down the lane, heads together again,
They came strolling along arm in arm.
'Billy-O,' I called out. He looked all about.
Breeda jumped with a squeal of alarm.
'I'm up here, you dunce.' 'Oh, how was the dance?'
'I haven't been in,' I replied.
'The guards came around, the escape route was found,

And the ladder is laid on its side.'
'Sure you're in a fine pickle,' said Bill with a giggle,
'You're lucky we came by at all.'
He pushed and I pulled till the ladder was hauled
Out of sight at the top of the wall.
I leapt through the air to a roof that was there
And wondered if all the Crew made it.
A voice made me freeze - 'Pint of Guinness, please.'
I saw it was Paddy who said it.
He sat in a trance, sadly wetting his pants,
So I let him continue his prattle.
I climbed down a tree to where I could see
That others had fallen in battle.
Young Thomas lay prone with his head on a stone,
Lovingly hugging his Jameson.
Two naked feet, like slabs of fat meat,
Stuck out of the hedge I found Seamus in.
I followed the trail of the heroes who fell
To the Quad, where the music was loud.
There stood, broadly grinning, surrounded by women,
The Limerick Rake, looking proud.
I was feeling much bolder, till a hand on my shoulder
Told me I was caught by police.
'Come with us, sir. We'd like an answer
As to how you got into this place.'
'Hold on,' said the Rake. 'You've made a mistake,
For I have his ticket with me.'
He reached in his pocket and pulled out a ducat
That made me both legal and free.
'Look here, my friend,' I said. 'You could have entered
This Ball by the main college gate.
So why did you call for a crawl up the wall,

When you already had tickets paid?'
The Rake laughed and said, with his hand on the head
Of a fox with a smile on her face,
'Now you know that the fun and the thrill of the hunt
Is not in the kill, but the chase.'
I left at five, and glad to survive.
Some never recovered at all.
For no one stayed sober the night we went over
The wall to the Trinity Ball.

'Buildering'

While the Trinity Ball has been the destination of most night climbers, it is far from the most exotic. In fact, the most fascinating climbing achievements have been performed once the climbers were already inside the walls of Trinity. The University Climbing Club records a series of adventurous climbs taken under cover of darkness within the College grounds. In the 1960s, the club became fascinated with climbing buildings, an activity referred to as 'buildering' by its members.

Several club members worked to construct a clandestine guidebook to methods of scaling the various edifices. Signed only with initials, these daredevils had no intention of their exploits leading them to fall afoul of the College authorities should the record of their adventures one day be seized. Yet their records, kept for posterity, reveal very clear instructions of how to scale landmarks such as the various quads, the Old Library, and the ornate Graduates Memorial Building (GMB). The guide also rates the difficulty of each climb, and sometimes includes strategies for quick exits.

The most impressive climb, and one of the most difficult, is the Campanile. This great bell-tower, constructed in 1853,

'Over the Wall to the Trinity Ball'. Richard Marsh's epic poem tells the story of students trying to steal into the Trinity Ball, an effort mirrored by many students with varying degrees of success over the years. (Liam Brophy)

commands the Front Square of the College. As Trinity's most iconic building, the Campanile has long been used as a symbol of the institution. The Climbing Club's records show minutely detailed instructions on climbing the bell-tower, ranking the climb as extremely difficult. No doubt the difficulty arose as much from the exposed position of the Campanile to the porters' lodge as to the sheer height and treacherous character of the granite facings. The first confirmed ascent of the Campanile took place in 1962. *Trinity News*, the student newspaper, records the sighting of a red top hat attached to the cross on the top of the Campanile. While not taking public credit for the climb, the Climbing Club states in its records for the year that the Campanile ascent was the session's 'crowning achievement'. For four days the top hat remained atop the Campanile and was only removed after College authorities arranged for scaffolding to be put up at considerable expense. A few members of the Climbing Club had publicly expressed their willingness to make the climb in the light of day to remove the offending hat, but were rebuffed by the authorities, who were not amused by the offer.

The Campanile was scaled twice more, in 1965. One of the climbs left another top hat, a black one this time. The other left a stuffed crocodile. *Trinity News* records that the fire brigade eventually had to be called in to remove the crocodile. Little documentary evidence exists for any later climbs, though there have been many students who have claimed to have braved its summit.

A first-hand witness to a 'buildering' attempt has been written by Jose Xuereb, who resided as a student in Trinity at the start of the 1960s. Jose was asleep late at night in his room when he was awakened by a rhythmic tapping on his window. This piqued his curiosity as the room was several stories up. Gazing out the window he was met with a rather surprising sight: 'On the ledge

The Campanile, the bell-tower which dominates Front Square. The campanile was the great challenge for those who braved the climbing of Trinity's many edifices under cover of night. (William Murphy)

outside were two brawny undergraduates in dark sweaters. A clear look through the reflecting glass showed them to be bedecked with ropes. They looked very suspicious, so I opened the window and asked them in'. The climbers explained that they had been climbing the face of the Front Square residence block when they were spotted by the porters and had been forced to bid a swift escape. Moments later a knock came at the door, and Jose's new friends swiftly hid under his bed while he answered, feigning drowsiness. The Junior Dean and a gang of porters were outside and not in a good mood. They insisted upon inspecting the apartment, and Jose was compelled to let them in. Fortunately for the climbers and their new accomplice, the porters saw nothing amiss and left for the night. Once the coast was clear, the climbers came back out and, after waiting for things to die down outside, made good their escape, through the door rather than the window.

GMB Ledge. The narrow ledges the builderers took to can cause vertigo in even the most seasoned rock climbers. (Aifric Ní Chríodáin)

Buildering Beyond Trinity

Some of the night climbers even took their skills outside of the College grounds, making mischief around Dublin. One famous incident of 'buildering' beyond the walls of Trinity took place in 1957, and involved three students attempting to gate-crash a party held by a student living off campus on behalf of the Laurentian Society. The party host was living in a three-storey townhouse with several other people. Scoping out the situation from below, the three plucky climbers decided that the best way to gain access would be to shimmy up the drainpipe and slip in through an open window on the top floor. At first, this plan worked quite well, as two of the young men made it up the drainpipe. However, when the third fellow was halfway up the pipe it came away from the wall, bringing the poor lad crashing down onto a skylight below, giving him a bit of a concussion and a cut hand. The three students might still have made good their escape had it not been for the unfortunate fact that the house they were raiding abutted the Embassy of the United Kingdom. This was the 1950s, and there was fear of the IRA attempting to attack the embassy. The Gardaí were summoned to the scene rapidly and the young men were apprehended. Fortunately for them, however, the officer questioning them realised they were not terrorists, but just stupid students. He was further softened by the fact these students were all members of the Dublin University Boat Club. As it transpired, the officer had been setting up a boat club in the city and had received help from the university club in getting it started. Because of this, the young men did not spend the night in jail but were instead returned to Trinity unscathed. It is hard to imagine students being given such leeway by the officers of the law nowadays.

Today, with the advent of CCTV and professional security guards, climbing the Campanile, and all buildings in and around the College, has become far more of a challenge. A further disincentive to latter-day night climbers is the increased concern for health and safety that has pervaded Trinity, and most of the Western world for that matter. Fear of expulsion, fierce censure, or even prosecution has served as sufficient disincentive to today's would-be buildering enthusiasts.

THE PRINCE OF MISCHIEF AND THE GREAT DEAN

The late 1950s saw the admittance to College of one of the most prolific pranksters and mischief-makers to ever grace the halls of Trinity. Andrew Bonar-Law, who would go on to be a noted expert in antiques, was the terror of the servants of order and discipline throughout his time as an undergraduate. As one of his many College friends, Dr I.K. Ferguson OBE (today a respected botanist), describes him, Andrew 'seemed to have the keys to most doors and gates, one was led to believe'. It appears he had the run of the College, and took all the liberties imaginable. The stories of his exploits are many and varied and make for fantastic storytelling.

The Phantom Organist

One exploit involved the tasteful disruption of a Commencement. As students, parents, and academics flowed into the Examination Hall for the solemn Latin ceremony, they were serenaded by the lovely music of Bach coming from the great organ balcony. At first, everyone thought someone was simply playing the organ, but this confused the Commencement organisers as no arrangement had been made for music of any kind, let alone an organist. The ceremony was about to begin, yet the music continued unabated. Climbing up to the balcony, the porters discovered no one seated at the organ, and were at a loss to determine where the music was coming from. After a brief search they discovered that a record-player had been secreted inside the organ and left to play. The record-player was promptly removed and the ceremony recommenced.

Even though he had got away, the College authorities knew well who had done the deed and sought young Master Bonar-Law out. Andrew commented on the aftermath of the incident, stating that the officials, 'made a very magnanimous gesture, in returning the record used – Bach's "Pascalia & Fugue" – giving thanks at the same time that "Jailhouse Rock" hadn't been the chosen record'. Of course, there was no chance Andrew would have chosen so offensive a record: he may have been a rascal, but he was also a gentleman.

Night-time Bricklaying

Another amazing incident occurred when Andrew and a friend, walking one night through the Front Square, serendipitously came across a pile of bricks and mortar, evidently left over from some repair or building project. Never a person to pass up a fabulous opportunity, Andrew quickly set about to mischief. The next morning his deeds became clear, as a student of the time, Beula Garcin, records: 'I arrived at the Reading Room one morning, to join a group that were unable to get into the building. The reason became apparent as I got to the steps. The door had been bricked up very artistically, leaving us

absolutely non-plussed'. Andrew's workmanship delayed many students from being able to continue their studies that day, but most of them, it seems, were willing to appreciate the sheer brazenness of the act. Workmen were quickly called in and the door was unblocked by the afternoon. But it served as a warning to the College not to leave items that might be put to unconventional use out over night.

The Trolley Car and the Examination Hall

Andrew Bonar-Law's greatest exploit, however, involved incredible tenacity, skill and planning. A professional crew had been in Trinity for some time filming a motion picture, and were using the picturesque Front Square as scenic

Postgraduate Reading Room. A study space for postgrad students, many were dismayed to find one day that the entrance had been bricked up one night as part of one of the most elaborate pranks committed in College. (Aifric Ní Chríodáin)

backdrop. The crew was using what was at the time a very sophisticated set-up, as I.K. Ferguson again recalls: 'They had a trolley like a large car-chassis on wheels of motor car size, on which they mounted the camera and the cameramen sat on and the camera could move in and out, etc., mounted on this'.

Over the long June bank holiday weekend, the camera crew departed for a short vacation, leaving the trolley-car parked in the Front Square. Seizing the incredible opportunity, Andrew proceeded to round up a crew of hardy and free-spirited lads, and led them out to the trolley-car under cover of darkness. They pulled the trolley across the square, and behind the Examination Hall. Andrew then led some of the group up to the roof, using keys mysteriously acquired. They lowered ropes down to the ground, which were then secured to the trolley-car. The merry crew then proceeded to hoist the trolley-car upward. Just when the car was nearly all the way up, it caught on a parapet, generating a loud grinding noise. The porters at the lodge were alerted by the sound and began a search of the Front Square. Before they could make a full circuit, however, Andrew and friends had already escaped across the roof and through a neighbouring apartment window, having left the trolley-car firmly fastened to the chimney of the hall, out of view of the casual searcher.

For a couple days the trolley car remained suspended there, in full view of one of the streets adjoining Trinity. Yet no one seemed to notice it and, after some planning, Andrew resolved to finish his prank. Rounding up another crew, he again gained clandestine access to the roof, where he and his fellow mischief-makers succeeded in hauling the trolley-car up onto the top of roof. They then positioned it just at the edge of the roof, facing out to the Front Square, where it would be visible to all once the sun rose. The next morning the College authorities were greeted with the sight of the trolley-car in full view.

Exam Hall Roof. Atop the roof was placed a car erstwhile used during a film shooting. Fetching it down proved a laborious and costly task.
(Aifric Ní Chríodáin)

Getting the trolley-car down proved a costly endeavour, and the work crew managed to damage a number of the roof slates, further increasing the already substantial headache paining the Trinity powers that be.

Enraged at the incident, the College disciplinarians tried to obtain evidence of the culprits, but none proved forthcoming, and though they had their perennial suspect in mind they could pin nothing on him.

Dr McDowell

Andrew Bonar-Law benefited during his time in Trinity from the presence of one of the most magnanimous Junior Deans in the College's long history. Dr R.B. McDowell was one of the most beloved figures in the College and served for thirteen years as Junior Dean, longer than any other. During his tenure,

R.B. McDowell developed a reputation for good-naturedness, and though he would enforce the rules when they were flagrantly abused, he was largely willing to let the students have their fun, within reason. He was even willing to help his charges out when they fell foul of the authorities in the outside world. As one former student fondly recollects, 'He twice bailed me out of the Garda pound where I'd been detained while the balance of my mind was fizzing with Guinness'. It seems small wonder he is remembered by those who knew him as a great Junior Dean.

One colourful story reflects well this sentiment. One day, Dr McDowell was strolling across the campus when he 'noticed a visitor, short of stature and walking with a peculiar gait, being accompanied by two undergraduates'. Intrigued, the Junior Dean walked up to the small party, and upon closer inspection discovered that the strange fellow was in fact a monkey. The owners pleaded with Dr McDowell to allow them to keep it overnight in their rooms. The Junior Dean agreed, having a great fondness for monkeys, on the condition that the monkey be removed from College the next morning. As it happened, the monkey did not much like the undergraduates' apartment and proceeded to go wild, smashing dishes and causing general mayhem. The students took the monkey to Dublin Zoo early the next morning.

Dr McDowell's easy-going nature was aided by a general sense of calmness in the student population during his tenure. The street battles, full-blown mayhem and flouting of authority that had so characterised previous centuries had long given way to gentler sentiments. Dr McDowell described the period as, 'an age when the undergraduate, generally speaking, took authority, paternal, school and academic, for granted'. In this atmosphere of acquiescence to authority, Dr McDowell did not have too many difficulties in

R.B. McDowell. The greatest Junior Dean of the twentieth century, perhaps ever, was much-loved by his charges, some of whom commissioned a portrait, now hanging in the rooms of the Historical Society. (Aifric Ní Chríodáin)

maintaining order, nor did he have much need of meting out harsh punishments. This was not always the case, however, and when students overstepped in their mischief, the Junior Dean could bring down the hammer.

Dr McDowell had a particular aversion to fireworks, which had become a fad in 1958 and 1959, and would punish harshly those he caught making use of them. One nasty incident involved 'an aspiring engineer and a chemically-inclined natural scientist', who set up a daring firecracker prank on the day of a Commencement. As one student of the time described the incident, the Junior Dean and the porters raced around, 'hunting down fire crackers that had been placed strategically around College and fused to go off every twenty minutes or so for a number of hours'. The culprits were caught, and the pair was suspended for a term for their shenanigans. Dr McDowell would later comment, 'Getting drunk or going to bed with a woman is one thing, but fireworks are just childish'.

While he rarely showed it, the kindly Junior Dean had a core of steel that was best not messed with. This countenance came out in full force one hot day in May 1968. It was near the endpoint of the exam season, and most students were still hard at work cramming for their last few finals. Some lucky students had already finished, and a few of this sort were heading home in the afternoon after a day of heavy celebratory drinking. They were quite loud and rowdy, and as they passed through Botany Bay they disturbed many of the ardent studiers, whose windows stood open to fight the heat. Some of these studiers shouted down at the revellers to be quiet.

Fuelled by drink, the lads below proceeded to shout abuse up at their studious fellows. A few of the angrier students retaliated by upending buckets of water onto the heads of those below. The situation escalated rapidly and, within a matter of minutes, had become a full-blown riot on the square, with as many as 300 over-stressed undergraduates participating. One of these managed to set off a massive smoke bomb, which filled the entire square with acrid smoke. A porter, seeing only the looming smoke cloud and thinking a fire was in progress, swiftly rang the fire brigade, which arrived in force soon after. The College quickly descended into complete mayhem. And into this maelstrom strode the Junior Dean.

Summoned by the commotion, Dr McDowell had arrived in his guise of war god. An echoing cry of 'JD!' rippled through the crowd. As one witness to the nascent riot later described the scene, 'The JD didn't utter a word – then, or later. He did not need to. His simple presence defused the tension, and the Dublin Fire Brigade disappeared as quickly as it had arrived and, miraculously, College returned to normal inside a few minutes'. Truly, Dr McDowell in his warrior aspect was a force to be reckoned with, even if it was displayed only occasionally.

Andrew Bonar-Law succeeded in pulling off most of his spectacular stunts under the nose of the Junior Dean. Dr McDowell even commended the brilliance of the trolley-car incident. The nearest the young miscreant came to being apprehended was during yet another incident on the roof of the Examination Hall. Again, having enlisted a crew of mischief-makers, Andrew had carried what he later described as a 'self-standing "No Parking" sign about four foot tall' out to the edge of the roof and lowered it down in front of the hall with ropes. Just as they had detached the ropes and pulled them back out of sight, lo and behold Dr McDowell came puttering into view. The Junior Dean was well known for his eccentricities, including the habit of walking about the College, often at odd hours, pursuing circuitous and often overlapping paths. Preoccupied with his own thoughts, Dr McDowell walked past the Exam Hall several times, and apparently not realising the 'No Parking' sign did not belong where it had been laid. The pranksters did not move a muscle for fear of drawing attention to them. Bonar-Law later reflected on the incident, saying, 'The climbers simply sat, with their legs hanging over the ledge, hoping that he wouldn't look up'. Fortunately for them, the Junior Dean did not once gaze upward and, after a few minutes of seemingly aimless strolling, proceeded to amble off back toward his rooms. Andrew Bonar-Law had escaped detection yet again.

Since that time there has never been anyone to take up the mantle of prankster-in-chief, and Andrew Bonar-Law's shoes remain to this day tragically unfilled. Yet if someone were willing to follow in his mischievous footsteps, no doubt he or she would face far sterner opposition from the less amenable Junior Deans of the present age.

TEN

THE WOMEN OF TRINITY

Clandestine Visits

Trinity has had a long and fractious relationship with women. For its first 300 years, College was a bastion of male supremacy. The first interactions between members of the College and women were generally clandestine. Trinity was for most of its early centuries ostensibly women-free, with no ladies allowed to take degrees or serve in any capacity other than as custodial staff. The Fellows were even expected, until the nineteenth century, to maintain strict celibacy. Yet young men proved unwilling to part with feminine company so easily and contrived many ways by which to surreptitiously get their lady friends within the College gates for a bit of alone time. One such means employed during the eighteenth and nineteenth centuries was to have girlfriends dress in the garb of, and associate with, the washerwomen who came and went as employees of the College. In so doing, young ladies could come and go from students' rooms without causing any suspicion on the part of the porters tasked with keeping the genders strictly segregated. One enterprising undergraduate during the eighteenth century, who happened to have his lodgings in a ground-floor apartment in College, contrived to cut a hole in the floor of his bedroom and to build a rudimentary trapdoor, so that he could hide his lady callers easily if cornered by an unexpected inspection.

Female Students

At the end of the nineteenth century a movement began pressing for the admission of members of the fairer sex into the College. In 1892 a petition was signed by 10,000 women, demanding the opening up of Trinity's hallowed halls to all. Their efforts met initially with fierce resistance from the College Board, particularly the deeply conservative Provost George Salmon, who considered a university educated woman to be most unseemly and undesirable. The greatest fear was that young women might be able to mix with the young gentlemen of the College in an unregulated, very dangerous fashion were they to be admitted to study. Who knew what naughty behaviour they might indulge in behind the backs of the fellows and porters? In 1895 The Board stated emphatically this position in a public message, claiming that, 'If a female had once passed the gate … it would be practically impossible to watch what buildings or what chambers she might enter, or how long she might remain there'. This panic over girls' chastity was common, not only among the dons of Trinity, but across much of society in Ireland and the United Kingdom. Yet this view gradually softened under the relentless pressure of politically engaged women across the island, and the Board was finally forced to relent in 1904 when it received 'royal letters patent permitting women to receive degrees in the University of Dublin' from the Lord Lieutenant of Ireland, the King's chief representative. It admitted women for the first time as full members of the College that year and shortly thereafter awarded honorary degrees to three of the great female intellectuals of the time: Isabella Mulvany, Sophie Bryant, and Jane Barlow. By admitting women, Trinity became the first of the ancient universities of the British Isles to become a mixed campus. Oxford would follow suit in 1920 and Cambridge not until 1947.

Yet the progressiveness of Trinity's admissions policy was not strong enough to end all discrimination against women within the College. Well into the 1960s, female students were not allowed to be on campus after six in the evening (unless signed in with the porters, and then only for specific meetings or to go to library), to eat at the formal Commons

The Anti-Women Establishment. Provost Salmon represented the last opposition in the College establishment against the admission of women. Eventually his hand was forced to begin the process of admitting women. (Aifric Ní Chríodáin)

dinners, or to be elected Fellows. While technically full members of the College and able to take degrees, they were very much second-class citizens. One of the major symbols of this difference, one that has remained stubbornly fixed in practice to this day, is the wearing of mortarboard caps by females at their undergraduate Commencement ceremonies. While today they are worn purely as a matter of tradition, they were originally intended to symbolize the 'capping off' of the female education, since postgraduate study must surely be the province only of the superior male mind. While some graduates refuse to wear the cap on principle for this reason, most are happy enough to engage in the traditional sartorial pageantry.

The restrictions on female students' movements within College were subject to frequent disobedience. Stories abound of young ladies being chased through the squares and across the greens by the porters after being spotted after hours. One particularly lurid tale from the early 1900s, recorded in *TCD: A College Miscellany,* describes a young woman getting caught by the porters while hiding out in a tree. Women's movements were also restricted insofar as they were banned from entering the rooms of male students, a restriction that would not be lifted until the late 1960s, when the era of sexual liberation managed to wash over even the most rarefied of Trinity's traditions.

A male graduate of the 1960s recounts a tale in which he had had his girlfriend over for lunch in his rooms in Botany Bay, having surreptitiously spirited her into his apartment. While they were in the midst of preparing the meal there came a knock at the door and a call from outside declaring the visitor as an assistant junior dean on a surprise inspection. Thinking swiftly, the young man hid his paramour under his bed. The inspector was not particularly interested in his job and was quickly gone, leaving the young lovers in peace. Yet such rule-breakers had to be constantly on their guard lest they be caught by the authorities, since discovery could yield hefty punishments.

Female Invasions

Women were further discriminated against for many years by the old societies, particularly the Phil and the Hist. These ancient debating societies proved extraordinarily resilient to the changing landscape of Trinity and managed to maintain their rooms as a sort of segregated club for a long time. But the wave of change that was the 1960s struck them too. For much of the decade, the societies' old guard fended off attacks not only by the progressive voting members, but also from the frequent 'invasions' by female students into the all-male proceedings.

These impromptu political actions resulted in much mayhem, and the complete breakdown of many debates. Seeing the tide of history crashing down on them, the Phil managed to secure a vote in favour of admitting women in 1968. The vote was carefully timed by the progressive activists so as to coincide with a major boat club event, at which many of the more conservative members were in attendance.

Returning from their revels quite inebriated on the night of the vote, the boat club members were horrified to see their society irrevocably changed. The then-president and secretary resigned in disgust but the change stuck. A few female students, having heard that the vote was on, hid in the College rose garden late into the night. When women were declared eligible, they made a break from the garden to the Phil common room, dodging the porters along the way. They managed to pay their dues and receive their membership cards before the porters caught up with them and escorted them off the premises.

In 1969 the Hist followed the Phil's example and admitted women as well. Since then, women have found not just acceptance in the old societies, but great success. Both have had significant female representation on their committees. In fact, the first female Deputy Prime Minister of Ireland, Mary Harney, was Auditor, or chairperson, of the Hist in 1974.

The glass ceiling imposed upon the women of Trinity has largely been splintered over the past few decades. Today, more than half of the students and academic staff in College are female. So while George Salmon may be rolling in his grave, Trinity has moved with the times and continued a tradition of excellence, now thankfully extended to all citizens.

ELEVEN

ANCIENT RIVALRY, MODERN MISCHIEF: THE OLD SOCIETIES OF COLLEGE

Trinity is home to some of the oldest student societies in the world. Its fencing club, which has existed in various forms since the eighteenth century, began as a 'Gentleman's Club of the Sword' with the express purpose of instructing students in the art of duelling. Yet while the club has moved on to become Trinity's most successful sports team, many of the oldest student societies in the College remain firmly planted in tradition. Chief among the 'old societies' are the Philosophical Society and the Historical Society, and their rivalry has spanned nearly two centuries.

The Historical Society, colloquially known as the Hist, is the world's oldest student society. Founded in 1770 as a debating society, it has sought to maintain that tradition through the centuries. Many noted figures in Irish and British history are counted amongst its past membership, including the revolutionaries Theobald Wolfe Tone and Robert Emmet. Other public figures who began their careers in the Hist include Edward Carson, Brian Lenihan Jr, Ernest Walton and Bram Stoker. With thousands of members on its rolls, the Hist remains one of the largest societies in Trinity.

Every week, the Hist hosts debates on an array of subjects, featuring both student and professional speakers. The Hist is known for its rigid adherence to tradition, and often faces the criticism of being a closed-shop busier with navel-gazing than generating new ideas. The Laws of the Society, the Hist's governing constitution, is shown a level of reverence by some members usually reserved for holy books. This obsession with rules, regulations and traditions is appealing to some sorts of people, but most students of the College, even those who are members of the society, can find it somewhat unsettling, which is hardly surprising. The prestige of the organisation still allows it to coax excellent guest speakers to attend debates, which has been reason enough for many to join, even if they have little interest in its internal politics.

On the opposite end of the personality spectrum is the Philosophical Society, known by its members as the Phil. Founded in 1843 as the Dublin Philosophical Society, it originally served as a club for undergraduates, since the Hist was at that time dominated by postgraduate students. Since its founding, the Phil has been home to many prominent people, including Oscar Wilde, Bram Stoker (also of the Hist), Samuel Beckett and Senator David Norris. The Phil originated as a paper-reading society and is in fact the world's oldest such society, with its weekly meetings consisting of a paper being delivered to the society by a student or public figure of note followed by a debate on the paper's topic. In recent years the papers have largely been eschewed in favour of pure debates, making the formal difference between itself and the Hist quite scant.

Yet the Phil is the yin to the Hist's yang. Where the Hist's activities are often dominated by procedure and close adherence to tradition, the Phil has made a tradition of defying tradition. The Phil has a set of Laws very similar on paper to that of the Hist, having based them on that of the older society, yet they are rarely considered anything other than a guideline. If the elected council, which leads the Phil's daily activities, decides something would be enjoyable for the members, then fun comes first. This difference in opinion reflects itself in the sorts of people who join each society. While the majority of undergraduates are in fact paying members of both societies, if they choose to be involved in one of them it is traditionally (though not always) at the expense of the other. The Hist attracts people who admire its traditions and history, and who want to have serious, intellectual debates, making them generally of a more serious bent. The Phil, on the other hand, attracts the fun-lovers for whom the traditions and age of the society are incidental. Phil debates tend to be light-hearted and more concerned with oratorical spectacle than argument. Thus, while on paper the two societies appear virtually the same, their characters could hardly be more different.

The Phil and Hist, as the two longest-lived and most prestigious societies in College, have a special place in Trinity. They conjointly own a large neo-Gothic Victorian building in the Front Square of College. The Graduates' Memorial Building (GMB), completed in 1904, is the only student-owned building on a university campus in Ireland. The societies have the run of the building, on condition that they share its use with other clubs and societies and respect the rules and regulations of Trinity security. In spite of the sometimes stringent security restrictions imposed on them, the Phil and Hist enjoy a remarkable degree of autonomy from the rest of the College.

Over the years, the Phil and Hist have developed a long-standing rivalry, one that usually manifests itself in a friendly way, but can occasionally flare up into outright antipathy. Traditionally, both societies refuse to refer to the other by name during their

Completed in 1904, the Graduates' Memorial Building houses Trinity's
oldest organisations, the Philosophical and Historical Societies.
(Aifric Ní Chríodáin)

respective formal meetings, instead using the sobriquet 'the Other Society'. This rule has fallen into disuse of late, though some of the more stalwart Hist members refuse to change with the times.

Revenge is Sweet

The stories of the pranks pulled in the GMB are numerous, and some certainly go down in history as among the best ever pulled in Trinity. These pranks have traditionally been quite one-sided. The Phil has always been able to outdo the Hist when it comes to mischief, and when the Hist has tried to retaliate it has generally come out the worse for it. A recent example of this sort of escalation took place in 2011, during Freshers' Week, the period just before the academic year begins when new students go through orientation and are enticed by the various societies and clubs to join them. Some members of the Hist decided it would be hilarious to steal the Phil's lectern, from which participants in its debates always speak. They came under cover of darkness and hauled the lectern, a very heavy piece of hardwood, out of the GMB and over to one of the member's apartments. Upon realising the theft the next morning, the dedicated members of the Phil saw no option but to retaliate. A small team swept in that night to find some way of get back at their rivals, only to discover that the Hist had foolishly left the door to its committee room, where its library and administrative office is located, unlocked. Seizing the amazing opportunity, the Phil members proceeded to turn everything in the room upside-down. This included turning all of the furniture over, opening the bookcases and carefully flipping each of the hundreds of volumes on their heads, and flipping

Committee Room, the Hist's main workspace, has fallen prey to the Phil's prankery, suffering rearrangement and outright theft. (Aifric Ní Chríodáin)

the various portraits on the walls. They even turned the coat-stand over and methodically turned every item of clothing on it inside-out before hanging them carefully back onto the stand. The operation took a couple hours to execute, but such was the dedication of those in pursuit of vengeance. The Hist committee, arriving the next morning to see the utter shambles in which their room lay, chose surrender over further escalation. But that merely ended one skirmish. The war was not over, indeed, it could never truly end.

The Ballot Box

The Phil's long-time favourite prank involves the Hist's ballot box. This large wooden box was gifted to the Hist in 1903, and has served since that time as the society's podium during debates. The Hist has developed a firm attachment to the ballot box as one of its many historical relics. This attachment has led the Phil to create its own tradition of stealing the ballot box at every available opportunity.

Often times this simply takes the form of Phil members opportunistically snatching it up when left unguarded and bringing it back to their own rooms as a spoils of war. Inevitably the Hist come searching and demand to root through the Phil's possessions until they find it in whatever imaginative hiding place has been devised. Because the prank has been used repeatedly for over a century, Phil members have often become bored with the traditional hide-and-seek. To jazz things up they have come up with a number of variations of the tried and true joke.

One involved stealing the ballot box in the run-up to Christmas and wrapping it in gift paper before covertly placing it among other decorative presents under the Christmas tree in the Hist common room. The Hist committee spent many days searching for the ballot box and became quite distressed when it could not be found. The auditor (basically the president)

One of the Hist's most treasured artifacts, the Ballot Box has become a major target of Phil-led pranks over the years. (Aifric Ní Chríodáin)

of the Hist even threatened to get the Gardaí involved. This caused the hiders to relent and show them that it had in fact been in the Hist's possession the whole time.

Perhaps the most audacious plan devised for the ballot box was, alas, never executed. Some Phil members got very far into the planning stages of an elaborate scheme in which they would vacuum seal the ballot box in saran-wrap before encasing it in jelly.

The plan hit a snag when a large enough jelly mould could not be procured, and was eventually abandoned. Had it gone ahead, it no doubt would have been the crowning glory of the old running prank.

Professor Dumbledore

Enjoying pranks beyond thievery, the Phil has also, at times, seized the opportunity to disrupt the Hist's weekly debates with hilarious interventions. One memorable interruption involved a visit to the Phil by Michael Gambon, Dumbledore himself. After giving a talk to the Phil's members, the officers of the society invited him back to their rooms for drinks. It so happened that at the same time the Hist was holding a debate. The debating chamber of the GMB is a beautiful, echoing room, and is equipped with a lovely balcony that is attached directly to one of the Phil's rooms. After being told by several members of the Hist committee to be quiet because the drinks reception was disturbing the debate, the Phil hatched a plan, and even convinced their famous guest to take part. Striding out onto the balcony while a student was in the middle of a speech, Michael Gambon leered down at the assembled crowd and shouted, 'Would you kindly shut the fuck up!' before slamming the door and returning to the Phil's room to rapturous applause. To say the least, the Hist's leadership were not at all pleased to have been told off by Prof. Dumbledore.

The Faux-Jamaican

The most remarkable disruption of the Hist's debates, however, took place in 1973. The Hist was holding a debate on nationalism and were looking for an appropriate guest chair. It so happened that around the same time the correspondence secretary, the committee member responsible for organising the debates, had been contacted by one Comrade Odinga, a Jamaican radical politician living in exile in England. Comrade Odinga was very interested in chairing the debate, and agreed to come over to Dublin. The night of the debate, the chair arrived, clad in traditional Jamaican garb, and was invited to take the chair at the start of the debate. It took some time for the penny to drop, but eventually the Hist committee realised that their chair was not in fact Jamaican at all, but was rather an Irish man in elaborate costume, including a remarkable make-up job. Recognising the ruse, the committee promptly demanded that 'Comrade Odinga' vacate the chair, and the faux-Jamaican was escorted from the premises. As it turned out, Odinga had no connection to Jamaica whatsoever, but was rather an old member of the Phil named Hosford Turner who had been co-opted by the current leadership to participate in the elaborate ruse. Since then, the Hist has been far more careful in its choice of guests.

Election Mischief

The Phil has also, over the years, exploited the Hist's own rigid procedures to cause mayhem. The Hist has strict electoral rules that forbid the solicitation of votes. The expectation is that candidates for election to the committee will comport themselves as gentlemen (or ladies) and maintain silence on the issue of the elections. In 1989 the Phil saw a golden opportunity. In the election for auditor, only one candidate, Orla Corrigan, was standing. She had been on the committee for two years and was committed to the society. Rather than allow her to be elected unopposed, the Phil put forward its own candidate, John Smyth, who had been president of the Phil the previous year. Having no compunction to respect the rules governing the election, Smyth and his friends proceeded to quietly canvass the electorate. On Election Day, when the ballots were counted, Smyth, the former Phil president and long-time antagonist of the Hist, lost by a single vote. The close call that nearly saw an enemy elected as its head caused the Hist to embark on a re-evaluation of their electoral rules. But as is so often the case with the society, the demands of tradition won out and the rules remained largely unchanged. Since then, no one has attempted another soft coup, but it is a possibility of which the Hist is now ever wary.

The Prank that Rewrote History

While there are many great pranks to choose from, certainly one stands out from the rest, not for its disruptiveness or instant hilarity, but for its success in effectively rewriting history. In the 1990s, a Phil president realised that there was once an organisation called the Dublin Philosophical Society, founded in 1683 by William Molyneux. Conceived as an Irish equivalent of the Royal Society in London, this older society's membership included many of the leading lights of the time, including William Petty and Bishop George Berkeley. The society existed off and on for a number of years, dissolving finally in 1708.

Some of the former members of the society would later go on to found the Royal Dublin Society (RDS), which continues to this day. The president decided that he could single-handedly rewrite history, and cause significant upset to the Hist. The Phil proceeded to declare that it was in fact the natural successor of the Dublin Philosophical Society, and claimed, with no corroborating evidence, that it had been members of the RDS that helped set up the Phil in 1843. The president set the new founding date of the Phil as 1683 and never looked back.

Founding Dates. The Phil significantly exaggerates its age, claiming a founding date of 1683, whereas it was actually founded in 1843. This dating has caused the Hist no small amount of headache, which continues to try to make its greater age known. (University Philosophical Society)

Today, the Phil continues to use this much earlier, and historically outrageous date, and it is now looked upon as virtually heretical for a member to suggest that it may be less than accurate. The event is remembered by those who were members at the time as 'the Great Leap Forward'.

The Hist committee, upon hearing their society was no longer the oldest student society in the world, were livid. They took the matter to the College authorities, but no one but they really cared. While the University Calendar, which is the official book of all rules and regulations in the College, does not recognise the older date, the majority of the College community has come to accept the Phil's avowed founding date. All this argument over founding dates may seem academic and even childish to an outsider, but to the Hist it is deadly serious. What began as little more than a joke has evolved into one of the most contentious issues between the two societies, and has generated much enmity from the Hist traditionalists who see their rightful place and history being usurped.

The Phil and the Hist are woven indelibly into the fabric of Trinity College. They have been the playgrounds of some of Ireland's most distinguished sons and daughters and continue to have relevance today. That special place in Ireland's development and future is all the more hilarious when you consider how much time those future leaders must have wasted trying to one-up their great rivals.

TWELVE

IF YOU CAN'T WIN, STEAL

The University Philosophical Society, or the Phil as it is generally known, has long had a tradition of stealing the precious items of other universities when its members go abroad, often in the course of debating competitions. The tradition passed down in the society from the older members to the new recruits is simple: 'If you can't win, steal'. This maxim has led the Phil to embark on some remarkable feats of thievery in pursuit of a mischievous good time.

When Phil debaters leave the hallowed halls of Trinity and enter another university, they immediately begin scoping out the angles of possible theft. Many small items have been purloined by these ardent souls over the years, and are kept lovingly in the care of the society. These have included snooker balls taken from the Durham Union, a sign taken expertly off the wall of a building at Dublin City University, and even an 1843 edition of *Punch* from the Oxford Union. But these are relatively small stuff, and the Phil's aim is always to get something that is of sentimental value and that will thus be missed and sought after. One such item was the official gavel of the University of Limerick Debating Society, which was taken by one sticky-fingered Phil member while its guardian, the auditor of the society, was being distracted with strong drink. A similar fate met the official timing bell of the University College Dublin Literary & Historical Society, and the official membership book of the Philosophical Society of University College Cork.

In the cases of Cork and Limerick, the thieves were forced to return the goods or else the Phil would face banishment from the annual competitions held by those societies. Another interesting item acquired over the years was an elaborate gong, lifted from the music department of the School of Oriental and African Studies in London. The gong was used for a while to signal the entrance of the Phil's officers at the start of a debate, but was eventually broken after overzealous use. All of these thefts are taken in the spirit of fun, and it has become something of a game between the Phil and the various other debating societies around Ireland and the United Kingdom to see who can steal most from whom.

The President's Chair

One remarkable heist attempt happened during a visit to the Cambridge Union. At night, when most of the people at the gathering were heavily intoxicated, an intrepid band of Phil members grabbed hold of the elaborate throne-like chair of the Union president and carried it off into the night. It is unclear what they intended to do with the chair, as it could hardly fit on the plane back to Dublin, but that matter was settled when the disgruntled Union security guards came bounding down the street after them. The self-appointed spokesman of the thieves informed the guards that, while it might seem to an untrained eye that what they were doing was illegal (being theft), it was not the case, because it was an act taken purely to cause mirth, which he argued it clearly had. The guards proved thoroughly unconvinced by this line of argument so, abandoning the chair where it was, in the middle of the road, the burglars fled into the darkness and made good their escape.

The Cambridge Union. As opulent a structure as the Oxford Union, Cambridge enjoys a massive amount of prestige and wealth. When Trinity students visit they do their best to get one up on their English counterparts, or at least to knock them down a peg. (Wikimedia Commons)

The great wood chair of the President of the Cambridge Union proved too great prize for the lads of Trinity to make off with. (Wikimedia Commons)

Gladstone's Portrait

One heist stands above all the rest. In the early 2000s, a delegation from the Phil was attending a debating competition in the Oxford Union. The Union building is a massive, opulent place, with marble staircases, and furnished beautifully with books and art. It proved to be an irresistible temptation to the Phil. One of the rooms in the Oxford Union is called the Gladstone Room, so named because of the large and elegant portrait of the former Prime Minister that hung on its wall. The Phil contrived to steal this old and expensive portrait and to add it to their collection of stolen goods back in Dublin. Security during the competition was lax, as the Oxonians hardly expected anyone to be as brazen as to make off with anything truly valuable. But they were not counting on the Phil.

After a brief period of planning, the chosen thieves from among the Phil stole into the Gladstone Room, leaving a lookout on the landing, and gingerly removed the painting from the wall. They were about to make their way out of the building with Gladstone when a group of Oxonians came into view. Thinking quickly they stuffed the painting under a coat. However, despite their very best efforts the Phil were caught in this attempt to remove Gladstone and were forced to return home empty-handed.

The initial failure to liberate Gladstone from the Oxford Union only served to embolden the more ardent members of the Phil, and they came back to Oxford the next year promising to take the painting or die in the attempt. Choosing their time to strike carefully, they waited for everyone else in the Union to get thoroughly inebriated. When they thought the coast was clear, the intrepid Phil members silently entered the Gladstone Room in search of their prize. Yet to their horror Gladstone had

The Oxford Union. Oxford has been a major victim of Trinity-led pranking. Making off with a painting of Gladstone proved a step too far and resulted in the Phil nearly facing legal action. (Tony Hisgett)

been securely screwed into the wall so as to deny any hope of a repetition of the previous year. Despondent, the would-be art thieves left the room shamefaced.

The story might have ended there had not Providence intervened on behalf of the Phil. One of the erstwhile conspirators, while relieving himself in the Union's toilet, discovered on the windowsill a screwdriver. No doubt left there by some member of the custodial staff, the young and daring student concluded that it was a sign from Heaven demanding that their mission continue. He re-gathered his crew and made hastily back to the Gladstone Room where their prize beckoned.

Removing the painting without incident, they gently wrapped it in sheets acquired from the unguarded linen closet. Once secured, two of them lifted up the painting and proceeded to walk right out the front door unchallenged. The culprits headed immediately for the bus and took it to the ferry port, where they were able to transport the painting without fear of airport customs causing them worry. The plan seemed to go without a hitch and the painting was safely brought back to the Phil's rooms in the Graduates' Memorial Building. The Phil celebrated the victory as its most spectacular ever, and everyone was most pleased with the stunning achievement over the Oxford lot.

But the story did not end there. After all, a very valuable piece of art had just been stolen from the Oxford Union and transported across international borders. In their eagerness for mischief the Phil had found itself in rather dicey legal waters.

This fact was made very plain when the president of the Phil received an email from his counterpart in Oxford. The correspondence itself no longer exists, but the records of the Phil describe the message to have been to the effect that there had once been a room in the Oxford Union called the Gladstone Room and which was now simply The Room. The Oxford president suggested that the Phil might have some inkling of where the painting had wandered off to, and that should the painting be returned within a couple days the Oxford Union would not have to begin the process of filing with the insurance company. He also remarked that, given the financial and historical value of the painting, he would be compelled by the insurance agreement to contact Interpol about the affair. Catching the Union president's meaning, and recognising the fact that they had best comply, the erstwhile heroic-lead thief found himself climbing aboard the next ferry back to England. Arriving at the Oxford Union, he handed the painting back into the hands of its rightful owners and then bid a hasty retreat home. Thus the Phil managed to accomplish an impressive international art heist, and to avoid a potential diplomatic incident all in one go.

The Dangers of Leaving Your Computer Unguarded

Not long after the second Gladstone incident the Phil attended an intercollegiate meeting at the Cambridge Union. Much the same as its Oxford counterpart, the Cambridge Union is technically a private members' club, and is housed in similarly opulent conditions. Located in downtown Cambridge, the Union building is a landmark of the city and the home of many precious objects, including artefacts and artwork bequeathed by its many wealthy and powerful past members. The event organizers, having heard along the grapevine and in Oxford's newspaper of the Gladstone painting's unfortunate adventures, decided to mitigate any damage the rowdy Trinity students might cause to their premises. Since the event was to take place over a weekend, the Cambridge people had to keep careful tabs on the visitors lest they try to make off with anything in the middle of the night. The solution they reached was ingenious in its simplicity: they locked the Phil delegation in the spacious office of the Union president, a fairly spartan workroom unadorned with anything easily removed, hidden or broken. The organizers softened the blow by offering the Irish a few bottles of spirits to enjoy during their internment. Apart from a few comments from the Phil about a repetition of Irish segregation, and one reference to the office as a 'new Australia', the visitors were satisfied with the proffered whiskey and comfortable sofas and carpeted floor.

Having imbibed heavily of the free drink, the young lads could not help but forget their promises of good behaviour. How could they allow the English to continue the long oppression of the Irish people? Their ancestors called for redress, and the Phil were happy to answer. They swiftly set about looking for some means of causing mischief against the ancient Oppressor. Yet after reconnoitring the room they found little opportunity for theft or mayhem. Left without any other option and despairing of their failure, they turned to washing away their sorrows once again with the dregs of their drink. But Fate was to intervene. One of the young men decided to check his email's before going to bed. The president's computer was on, and the student felt it would be only fair that he be free to make use of the Union's internet, since it had so far been so unaccommodating to his pranking spirit.

Sitting at the computer he discovered something amazing: the president's email account was still signed in and his online address book open. Such an opportunity comes rarely in a life and, having alerted his compatriots to the situation, he turned his attention to making full use of the boon before him. They deliberated over the best prank that they might perform and eventually settled on a doozy. They pasted the entire address book into an email and then sent an eclectic set of pornographic videos and images to everyone on the mailing list. For most people this sort of online prankery would be embarrassing in the extreme, with family, co-workers, and maybe a professor or two getting the email. In such cases the email might be easily explained and face quickly saved. Not so with the president of the Cambridge Union Society. On his mailing list were the email addresses of most members of the UK parliament, including the Prime Minister, the Queen, several other heads of state, and a few Nobel laureates. The nature of the prank was such that it took a couple days for the Union to realize what had happened and by then the damage was done, and the culprits safely back across the sea to Dublin. The Phil was temporarily banned from attending events at the Union, but has since been rehabilitated, though the presidents since have always been fastidious in their logging out.

Since the incidents of the Gladstone painting and Pornogate, the Phil has attempted to be more conservative in its playful games with other societies. But the spirit of mischief remains undimmed, and when the Phil comes to town, other college societies become extra vigilant.

THIRTEEN

ARENA OF MAYHEM: THE COLOURS DEBATES

In sport, proximity breeds rivalry. And the same is true of universities. Trinity's great rival is University College Dublin, usually called UCD. UCD, located south of the Dublin city centre in Belfield, is a fine academic institution, though it is the brave Trinity student who is willing to say so, especially when they are competing head to head in an intervarsity setting. For over a century, Trinity's favoured sons (and more recently daughters) have pitted themselves against their ancient foes.

Every year sporting events and other competitions are held between the students of the rival institutions, and much stock is put in the bragging rights victory brings. These 'colours' competitions are often popular spectator events because of the greater ferocity with which the players invariably compete. Many of these events have exciting histories, but none has generated more chaos than the Comedy Colours Debates.

Held for decades, the Comedy Colours Debates occur twice a year, usually within a couple weeks, one in Trinity and one in UCD. The debates share a similar format, with between three and four students from each college appointed as champions to defend their institutions' honour. These representatives are then pitted against each other, seeking to mock their opponents into oblivion. There is always technically a motion or resolution to be debated, but this is invariably ignored in favour of insults and abuse for the other side.

The Trinity debate tends to be the milder of the two, not because Trinity students are any less lively or willing to heckle than their purportedly unwashed and illiterate UCD counterparts, but because of the venue. The Trinity debate is held in the college's stately debating chamber, a beautifully apportioned room replete with massive portraits of illustrious graduates of past centuries. The result is a crowd that is willing to be boisterous, but not outright rampageous. The situation is quite different in UCD. The Belfield campus is a much newer, uglier place. The buildings are purely functional, with none of the elegance of Trinity's old structures. The debate in UCD has been held for the last few decades in one of the many large, cavernous lecture theatres. It is exactly because the venue in UCD is so functional that the students are more willing to cause havoc. The best stories, therefore, invariably come from the adventures of Trinity's champions who braved the road to UCD.

The insults thrown about in the Trinity debate tend to be fairly straightforward mockery of each other's institutions in a general sense, with the humour usually broad-based in its content and delivery. Not so the debate in UCD. There the battle takes on a very different character. In it, the UCD speakers take on the guise of rebels, the rightful heirs to the men of 1916, the embodiments of republicanism and the Catholic citizens of Ireland. The Trinity representatives in turn take on the personas of the Protestant Ascendancy, monarchists and unionists one and all. The Trinity speakers are usually chosen for their willingness to adopt this new identity and play it up for maximum comedic effect. This sectarian character adds a certain fuel to the fire, and the students in the audience tend to go quite mad, throwing food and other objects at the hated Trinity oppressors, and shouting so loudly that little of the actual debate is ever heard beyond the first few rows of seats.

The intensity of the debate in UCD was amplified over time, as a tradition developed wherein the speakers from Trinity sought to outdo themselves by increasing the level of mockery and the offensiveness of their adopted personas, while at the same time the debate organisers sought to rouse the audience to ever greater acts of carnage in order to increase the spectacle. This one-upmanship reached a fever pitch one day in the early 2000s.

After a few successive years in which students had brought more projectiles than ever before, including dozens of eggs, which resulted in massive cleaning bills, the UCD administrative department decided it was sick of paying for the aftermath of the yearly mayhem. The result was a significant increase in security surrounding the debate. As students arrived to watch they were stopped outside the door to the lecture theatre by college security guards who would confiscate anything that might be quickly turned into a messy projectile. Thus for a couple years the amount of mess did not correspond to the amount of abuse being verbally thrown, much to the chagrin of the students eager to pelt their hated rivals with garbage and foodstuffs. Some enterprising students still managed it; one convinced a guard that the large pumpkin he was carrying into the theatre was for his mother for Halloween (which was only a week away) and that he could not be separated from it, as he would get no end of abuse if he went home empty-handed.

The guard was nice enough to let him through. The student repaid the kindness by, literally seconds after stepping through the door, breaking the pumpkin over his knee and chucking its messy contents at the Trinity debaters seated at the bottom of the lecture theatre. After that incident, the security guards became even more vigilant.

With this in mind, the debate organisers set about a cunning plan to evade the watchful eye of the security staff. Deliberately booking a lecture theatre, which was not in use for any other purpose before the debate, the organisers entered the hall hours before the event was meant to kick off. They proceeded to tape dozens of boxes of eggs, as well as a number of super-soakers filled with a nasty mixture of water and lube, to the undersides of all the desks in the theatre, thus bypassing the security that would soon be screening people at the door. Word was quietly spread that the debate was going to reach a whole new level of carnage, and turn out that afternoon was massive. In a lecture theatre that could seat a few hundred, people were clogging all of the isles and even sitting on top of each other. Finding the promised ammunition under their desks, the UCD crowd got ready for a conflict like no other.

Meanwhile, the Trinity team had arrived in UCD a couple of hours early. The four young men chosen for this year's battle were some of the best ever put forward for the debate, largely because most of them more or less believed they were part of the landed gentry, and that everything in the country had gone to ruin after the Protestant Ascendancy came to an end. One of them even wore a Union Jack as a makeshift sash as part of his debating attire for the day. The team was taken to a side room to wait for the debate to begin. The room was furnished with snacks and drinks for the speakers, including two twenty-four-bottle cases of very cheap beer. Left alone in the room, the Trinity speakers quickly hid one of the cases from sight and began quickly drinking their way through the one still on the table. By the time the UCD team arrived they had polished off most of them. The UCD representatives asked where the other case of beer was, and the Trinity lads succeeded in feigning ignorance of its existence. While they continued to wait, the Trinity team took turns going to the bathroom where they would rush through some of the stolen beer. By the time they were called to the theatre, they had finished all forty-eight bottles between the four of them.

While the Trinity speakers busied themselves getting inebriated, the debate organisers took the time to get the crowd worked up into frenzy. They reminded the crowd of Trinity's history of snobbery and cursed their rival in colourful terms. The pre-debate pep rally ended with a chorus of Irish rebel songs. By the time the debate was ready to begin, everyone was riled up.

As soon as the Trinity team came out onto the theatre floor, now all bedecked with Union Jacks, the eggs came hurtling down. Expecting some abuse, the Trinity lads strode bravely through the maelstrom. The first Trinity speaker was called up to begin the debate, but before he even reached the podium he was struck in the side of the head with a large piece of fruit. He proceeded to call out the person in the front row he believed to have thrown the projectile, and in the ensuing altercation proceeded to be gently punched in the face. After this short tussle ended, the speaker still gave his speech, ripe with abuse for the crowd and all things UCD, but was drowned almost entirely by the nonstop catcalls and jeering from the crowd.

This intense noise would continue virtually nonstop for the entire event. The Trinity students gave the impression of being unfazed in the face of this incredible racket, and when it was the second speaker's turn to go up to the podium he got up and strode with solemn dignity through the hail of eggs and abuse. But as soon as he got up to the podium his entire demeanour changed. Rather than give a speech he climbed up onto the podium, turned around, dropped his pants and mooned the audience. Written across his buttocks in large letters was 'UVF'. This mocking reference to the Ulster Volunteer Force, the brutal Unionist paramilitary group, resulted in an uproar more intense than had ever been heard in a colours debate.

Clearly the Trinity team had come to put all past performances to shame. The third Trinity speaker seemed to be breaking from his predecessors and actually began to give a speech of sorts. But not long into his remarks he proceeded to mime an action as if cradling a sniper rifle in his hands, sweeping the crowd with his imaginary weapon. He then remarked, still squinting through the phantom scope, 'I haven't seen this many Fenians since I was looking down the barrel of my gun on Bloody Sunday'. Yet another joke calculated to produce maximum outrage and uproar. It took a long while to quiet the crowd enough for the debate to continue at all. By the time the final Trinity speaker rose to approach the podium, the theatre had descended into almost total anarchy. The organisers, having seen their event spiral well out of control, acted as best they could to keep things from spilling over into full-on violent conflict. The last speaker had a treacherous walk, as the floor was by this time slick with a layer of watery lubricant, and many of the spectators took the opportunity to hurl the last of their eggs. By some twist of fortune not a single egg managed to land on its target. Upon reaching the podium, the final champion of Trinity still standing proceeded to mock the audience for their lack of marksmanship. But this tempted fate and seconds after he spoke this challenge, the speaker was struck squarely in the face with an egg, yolk dripping down his face and onto his shirt.

When the debate finally came to an end, the lecture theatre looked like a warzone. The floor and walls were thoroughly coated in egg, lubricant, and other food and garbage, and the organisers had to work hard to clear the raucous crowd without any injuries. The Trinity representatives were invited to the college bar for a pint with the UCD team and the organisers, where they apologised for their taking the unionist gag perhaps a bit too far. They were told to think nothing of it, that in their position they would have done the exact same thing. Thus all fences were mended, until the next year of course.

But the story did not end there. Upon seeing the utter destruction wrought upon their lecture theatre, the UCD administration was livid. But they were enraged all the more when they were informed of the ribald behaviour of the Trinity students who had been invited to speak and had made light of atrocities. A complaint to Trinity resulted in the team being brought before the Junior Dean for a thorough dressing down. The young man who had painted the letters on his backside was in particularly hot water for exposing himself in public in addition to the insensitive message itself. He was threatened with serious punishment, perhaps even expulsion, for bringing the name of the College into such disrepute. Fortunately, the auditor of the Literary & Historical Society in UCD, which had been a sponsor of the debate, wrote to the Junior Dean in defence of the students involved. He explained that the whole event was, in fact, a massive piece of performance art and that the roles had been loosely scripted in advance. He went on to write that it was in this very particular context that the event took place, and that the audience of highly sophisticated and socially aware students not only expected, but demanded this remarkably clever and courageous satirical deconstruction of sectarianism.

Faced with this evidence, the Junior Dean was forced to relent, and the student was spared no greater punishment than a scolding. That fateful Colours Debate did have further consequences, however. After the insanity of the debate, the cleaning bill and the sectarian comedy, the UCD authorities took a much harsher stance on what the debate could include. Security then after was present in the lecture theatre for the debates. Thus the Colours Debates today, while still hilarious and full of mockery and wit, are far tamer than once they were.

FOURTEEN

MYTHS AND LEGENDS

A college as old as Trinity has a habit of gathering about itself a collection of fascinating myths and legends. The stories are often retold with complete seriousness, and enter the canon as true tales. Yet many of these stories have no basis in truth in the first place, or have faced so much embellishment in the retelling that they have lost all semblance of fact and descended into the realm of fancy.

The Campanile Curse

One of the most frequently told legends has become something of a superstition. The story goes that if an undergraduate passes under the Campanile, the imposing bell-tower dominating the Front Square, they will not pass their exams. There are many variations of this tale with some claiming that it is only when the bells are ringing that one should not pass under the Campanile. Others raise the stakes in the telling by claiming that should one pass under the Campanile (either ringing or not, depending on the teller) the student will never graduate at all. This story in all its various forms has been told and retold to the junior freshmen and it has taken on a powerful superstitious character. Were one to take a day to observe the comings and goings through Front Square, one would see that the only people passing under the Campanile are tourists unconcerned with the curse. Even the most sceptical students have decided to err on the side of caution and assiduously avoid passing under it.

Shooting Catholics

Another famous legend, one told by almost every tour guide passing through Trinity's walls, involves a specific window in Front Square, (no one can agree exactly which), from which a member of the College community may legally shoot Catholics. This story is usually told as being some mysterious loophole in Irish law, in which the old rules of Trinity somehow take precedence. This story is, of course, ridiculous, but the deadpan retelling by studiedly serious tour guides and peer mentors has generated an air of believability. Other versions of this tale abound, including a particularly colourful one that states that the weapon with which the unfortunate Catholics may be shot is a crossbow.

College Rules

Yet another story involving the antiquated rules of the College begins with a student arriving at the Examination Hall to sit his finals. As he sits down, he signals for a proctor to come over to him and proceeds to ask him when the refreshments will be served. The proctor informs the student that refreshments are not served during exams. The student responds by producing an old College rulebook detailing the right of a student to a glass of porter while sitting any and all examinations. Perturbed by this request, the proctor enlists the help of the Junior Dean who attempts to convince the student to just sit the exam and stop making silly requests. The student is unwilling to budge, saying he will not sit the exam until the proper refreshment is provided. The Junior Dean proceeds to leave the hall in a flurry and heads to the Old Library. Returning a brief while later, the Junior Dean congratulates the student on his prudent reading of the rules of the College and instructs the proctor to fetch a glass of porter for the young gentleman.

The Junior Dean then turns to the student and informs him that he is to be fined for having worn inappropriate attire to the exam. The student asks what is amiss about his clothes, which seem to him to be perfectly suitable for this occasion. The Junior Dean replies that the student has forgotten to wear his sword, a grave offense for a gentleman to commit.

The Exam Hall, the great examination chamber, has been the venue of many great legends.

Another, less believable version of this story ends with the Junior Dean saying that the absence of the student's sword is a death penalty offense, after which the student agrees that he really does not need a glass of porter after all. The best versions of this legend, as with all tall tales, are the ones that give convincing details in the telling. Some choice details thrown in to add credibility to this tale have included the age of the regulations, such as one telling that has it as the College Calendar of 1794. It has also been set in various times, ranging from the 1940s to the 1980s, depending, of course, on the teller.

The Bram Stoker Room

A rather interesting tale has also popped up regarding the allocation of rooms in the Graduates' Memorial Building. In 1903, the Philosophical and the Historical societies met and divvied up the rooms of the building mostly evenly, with the Hist getting one extra room as recompense for the fact that the Phil got control of the ground floor of the building (considered the choicer real estate by those involved).

This extra room, located on the third floor of the GMB, went through a number of uses over the years, at one time even being a dedicated smoking room, before becoming a society workspace. The room became known at some stage in the 1950s or '60s as the Bram Stoker Room, a name it has retained to this day. Today, the Bram Stoker Room belongs to the Phil. How the room changed hands has become a matter of legend. The story goes that in the late 1960s the president of the Phil and the auditor of the Hist became embroiled in a high-stakes card game in which the Hist auditor made a serious loss. Seeking to recoup his losses, but lacking any

Bram Stoker, the author of *Dracula*, was the only person to lead both the Hist and the Phil. (Wikimedia Commons)

more funds to wager, the auditor proceeded to put up ownership of the Bram Stoker Room as his bet. The president was quick to accept the wager and promptly beat the auditor once more, leaving the room in the permanent possession of the Phil.

There is no truth in this particular legend, though. The Phil did in fact acquire the room but by much more ingenious means than the legend tells. The truth of the matter is that when the Phil admitted women to become members in 1968, the Hist was still a fiercely all-male society. Suddenly inundated with new members the Phil needed more space. The Phil president prevailed upon the College Board and the Hist committee to give the Phil use of the Bram Stoker Room as a women's common room, since the Phil was in greater need of the space and the new women members apparently had special needs that necessitated a private common room of their own. The Hist acquiesced and the Bram Stoker Room was transformed into a ladies' reading room. This use would prove only temporary, as only a year or two later the room was changed back into a workroom, this time for the officers of the Phil. The Hist kicked up a fuss with the College authorities, but no one paid much attention. More than forty years on, the Phil retains the room and the Hist continues to fume about being swindled.

In truth, while the legends and stories that abound in Trinity are quite fun, they often pale in comparison to the real hijinks students have gotten up to.

EPILOGUE:
THE FUTURE
OF MISCHIEF

In 2011, pranks in Trinity College moved for the first time into the twenty-first century and cyber space. An enterprising individual, suspected to have been either a student or junior staff member, set about modifying the English Department website, adding to the staff listing one Conan T. Barbarian. The listing has been the only such direct attack on the College's website to date.

The elaborate entry refers to 'Dr. Conan T. Barbarian, B.A. (Cimmeria), Ph.D. (UCD), F.T.C.D. (Long Room Hub Associate Professor in Hyborian Studies and Tyrant Slaying)'. Sporting a photo of Arnold Swarzenegger taken from *Conan the Barbarian*, in which the future Governator starred as the eponymous warrior, the entry featured a course listing and College email address. The full biography of Dr Barbarian read as follows:

Dr. Conan T. Barbarian was ripped from his mother's womb on the corpse-strewn battlefields of his war-torn homeland, Cimmeria, and has been preparing for academic life ever since. A firm believer in the dictum that 'that which does not kill us makes us stronger', he took time out to avenge the death of his parents following a sojourn pursuing his strong interest in Post-

Colonial Theory at the Sorbonne. In between, he spent several years tethered to the fearsome 'Wheel of Pain', time which he now feels helped provide him with the mental discipline and sadomasochistic proclivities necessary to successfully tackle contemporary critical theory. He completed his PhD, entitled 'To Hear the Lamentation of their Women: Constructions of Masculinity in Contemporary Zamoran Literature' at UCD and was appointed to the School of English in 2006, after successfully decapitating his predecessor during a bloody battle which will long be remembered in legend and song. In 2011/12, he will be teaching on the following courses: 'The Relevance of Crom in the Modern World', 'Theories of Literature', 'Vengeance for Beginners', 'Deciphering the Riddle of Steel', and 'D.H. Lawrence'. He strongly objects to the terms of the Croke Park Agreement and the current trend of remaking 1980s films that he believes were perfectly good enough in the first place.

Conan T. Barbarian. The newest member of the English Department caused enormous consternation of the department heads and to the tech support people. (FansShare)

The prank made national news and even hit the international market after being picked up by the Associated Press. The embarrassed College administration made it clear that they would hunt down whoever had done it, and asserted a belief that it was an 'inside job' in the department, someone with access to the website's 'edits' page. Whoever it was who did it, they succeeded in opening a whole new chapter in the history of pranks in Trinity.

Thwarted by CCTV, more security, harsher restrictions, and more draconian punishments, the would-be prankster faces many more challenges than their predecessors in the fine art of mischief. Long gone are the days when Trinity students could voice their dissent from College directives with a well-placed bonfire or mass protest. Gone too is the opportunity for such daring feats as putting cars on rooftops or bricking up doors. The porters and security staff would surely stop such things before they could get under way and, if they could not, would certainly call the Gardaí to sort out the mess. It is no doubt good in some ways that students no longer have the full run of the College as they once did, but surely there must be room for some mischief still in this new millennium?

The creator of Dr Barbarian was truly an innovator, taking the realm of pranking from the physical world, where the odds have been so unjustly stacked against the mischief-maker, to the internet, where youthful exuberance and inventiveness still often reigns supreme. With such young minds still flourishing on campus, the future of pranks and mischief in Trinity College is bright indeed.

If you enjoyed this book, you may also be interested in …

1916 & All That

C.M. BOYLAN

This wonderfully irreverent take on
the history of Ireland. It will take you
from the 'Age of the Third Best Metal',
through the struggles of Wolfe Tone
(Ireland's best-named revolutionary),
right through the Celtic Tiger years, when there
was pancetta and rubies for all. And then on to
the present day, when there are fewer rubies.
And, on the way, this book is not afraid to ask
the hard questions, such as: Why were walls
so important for the Normans? And can you
describe and explain Limerick?

978 1 84588 749 0

Dublin Folk Tales

BRENDAN NOLAN

Do you know who the real Molly Malone
was, or the story of Marsh's Library, or
how the devil himself came to the Hellfire
Club? These and many more accounts of
Dubliners and Dublin City fill this book,
as told by Brendan Nolan, a professional
storyteller who has been recording these
tales for decades. These are the stories of
real Dublin, the stories that are passed from
generation to generation and which give this
city its unique character.

978 1 84588 728 5

**Visit our website and discover thousands of
other History Press books.**

www.thehistorypress.ie